The Rainbow Follows the Storm

Barbara,
Angel
Blessings!
Love,
Karen

THE RAINBOW FOLLOWS THE STORM

How to Obtain Inner Peace by Connecting with Angels and Deceased Loved Ones

KAREN NOE

BLUE DOLPHIN

Published by Blue Dolphin Publishing, Inc.
P.O. Box 8, Nevada City, CA 95959
Orders: 1-800-643-0765
Web: www.bluedolphinpublishing.com

ISBN: 1-57733-147-8

Library of Congress Cataloging-in-Publication Data

Noe, Karen, 1958-
    The rainbow follows the storm : how to obtain inner peace by
connecting with angels and deceased love ones / Karen Noe.
        p. cm
    ISBN 1-57733-147-8 (pbk. : alk. paper)
    1. Spiritualism. I. Title.

    BF1261.2.N64 2005
    133.9'1—dc22

                                                    2005008193

Printed in the United States of America

10   9   8   7   6   5   4   3   2

This book is dedicated to my mother,
Elise Christen,
my angel here on earth,
who has always been there for me.
I love you Mom!

Contents

Acknowledgments

I'd like to thank my family and friends who have graciously given me moral support when I was writing this book. Thanks so much to those who have allowed me to share their precious stories within these pages. Many thanks to Paul Clemens of Blue Dolphin Publishing who gave me the wonderful opportunity to get this message out there. Angel hugs to Dr. Doreen Virtue who came into my life after I had prayed to be guided to the right teacher who could show me what to do with the intuitive gifts I had suddenly been given. And, of course, a million thanks to God and His wonderful angels for pushing me to sit down and write what was needed.

Preface

The angels inspired me to write this book. At first I felt them gently guiding me to share my experiences with others. Then these feelings grew stronger as the weeks and months went by. In the midst of all these promptings, they started to give me signs, one of which was during a group meditation, with five of us holding hands in a circle. The last thing I remember is hearing someone scream. The next thing I recall is that I was lying on the floor with everyone staring down at me. The people in the group told me that an angel spoke through me, saying I needed to write this book and that if I didn't, I would choose to leave this earth because I wouldn't be doing what I came here to do.

This was something I couldn't ignore, and in my heart, I knew that it was true. I needed to get the message out, and I needed to do it as soon as possible. I wrote one paragraph, and for weeks didn't write anything else. Even though I knew I was supposed to write, I didn't know exactly what to write and didn't take the time to just sit down and do it. Then one night I was curled up on the sofa, moping around, knowing I should be writing, but not doing anything about it. Suddenly I felt an angel's presence, guiding me to get up and open up a book that was in the other room which I had purchased months earlier and hadn't even read yet. It was called, *The Earth, the Cosmos, and You: Revelations by Archangel Michael*. (In this book, Orpheus Phylos and Virginia Essene channel Archangel Michael.)

As soon as I picked up the book, I was specifically told to turn to pages 96 and 97, which I immediately did. I gasped as I began to read the words that were written upon those pages. Archangel Michael was speaking about people who are incarnated here from Andromeda. Yikes! There *was* such a place! (See chapter entitled "We Are One With the Universe" where I speak about receiving messages about Andromeda.) And that's not all.

He said, "Throughout various periods of time, many writers and philosophers have been given information to help change the consciousness within your planet. You may be one of those now awakening on the Earth plane who is experiencing an inner knowing that is vigorously motivating you to write and share your particular knowledge or expertise."

After I had read this, I just stood there dumbfounded. The angels then bestowed upon me a feeling of knowingness, as if they were speaking directly to me, and I began to sob. Okay, I was ready to really listen now. How could I not? I needed to write this book, and I needed to do it right away.

The main purpose of *The Rainbow Follows the Storm* is to prove that we are spiritual beings having a human experience, not the other way around. I am going to share with you many real stories of messages I have received from those who have crossed over to the other side. When I asked those for whom I received messages if I could include their stories in this book, they were all more than willing to allow me to share these experiences with you.

My wish for you is that, after reading this book, you too will experience the comfort of knowing that your soul truly is eternal. I've had the pleasure of receiving messages from those of all walks of life, as well as many from the animal kingdom. Some of the messages from the spirits who have crossed over came to those who didn't even know their loved ones had died until they went home and investigated further. This made the messages even more special to them because they realized these beings went out of their way to let them know that, although they had left their bodies, they were indeed still around and were okay.

I believe we all have the power to receive messages from the other side and have included a section to show you how you can receive messages yourself. All you need to do is be patient and allow the messages to come through easily and effortlessly. In other words, don't force anything to happen.

I've also included in this book chapters on various related topics, including one on God, one on healing, one on past lives, one on world peace, and even one about life on other planets and galaxies. Accept whatever feels right to you, and if anything does not, simply disregard it. I am not here to force my ideas upon you, but simply to share my experiences with you.

May peace and love be with you all! Please come now and enjoy the journey with me.

Introduction

I was sitting on the edge of my bed, suffering from a high fever and bronchitis, and was feeling very sorry for myself. Suddenly, a beautiful unforeseen white light snapped me out of my somber mood, as it mysteriously appeared in the room and slowly began floating towards me. It was unlike anything I had ever witnessed before. Somehow I knew I could speak directly to it, and silently demanded, "If you are not of God, you must leave!" In spite of my request, the light continued to move closer, and finally, it enveloped me, bestowing upon me a feeling of total peace, a tranquility that I had never felt before. The light then spoke directly to me in Italian, whispering, "Luce lucina, bella luce lucina." Since my grandparents were Italian and I had taken some Italian in school, I knew what the words meant: "Light, little light. Beautiful little light." I was speechless, and tears of joy began to roll down my face. Oh my God, I had just been touched by an angel! Little did I know that from that moment on, my life would never be the same again.

PART I

Opening up
to the
Spiritual Realm

CHAPTER 1

Opening up to the Psychic World

Now there are varieties of gifts, but the same Spirit; and there are varieties of service, but the same Lord: and there are varieties of activities, but it is the same God who activates all of them in everyone. To each is given the manifestation of the Spirit for the common good. To one is given through the Spirit the utterance of wisdom, and to another the utterance of knowledge according to the same Spirit, to another gifts of healing by one Spirit, to another the working of miracles, to another prophecy, to another the discernment of spirits, to another various kinds of tongues, to another the interpretation of tongues. All these are activated by one and the same Spirit, who allots to each one individually just as the Spirit chooses.

—1 Corinthians 12: 4-11 (NRSV)

I tried explaining to my family and friends about my experience with the light, but no one seemed to realize how it truly affected me. I began to experience a peacefulness and tranquility that I had never felt before and had an inner knowingness about things that previously I was not able to understand. Whereas before I had been searching for angels, now I *knew* them. Whereas before I heard about the oneness of everyone, now I felt this connectiveness of everything. All of a sudden, my priorities had changed. Before I was concerned about furnishing my house and acquiring things, and now they were the last thing on my mind. People who had known me for years could not believe I was the same person. And I really wasn't.

3

My psychic abilities also increased dramatically. At first, the messages I received from angels and departed loved ones started off slowly and in the most random places. A week after the "luce lucina" experience, when I was having breakfast at a local diner, I felt the angels urging me to talk to a woman who was sitting in the back room. I must admit, I was reluctant to do so, however, because I didn't even know her. Finally, when she was getting up to leave, I felt as if hands were pushing my back, forcing me to get up out of my chair to speak to her. I finally gave in, but as I approached her, I didn't even know what to say. I eventually acquired enough courage to tell her that I was able to receive messages from the angels, and that she should call me if she ever needed to talk. I then gave her my phone number and email address. I wasn't sure what she thought, and didn't hear from her for a while. I believed that she surely must have thought I was crazy!

About a month later, I received an email from this woman, asking me to go out to lunch with her because she had been very depressed and needed desperately to talk to someone. She wrote that her husband had drowned a few months earlier, her mother-in-law had also recently died, and she was just diagnosed with breast cancer.

"And by the way," she wrote me. "How the heck did you know I needed to talk?"

Smiling to myself, I emailed her back, and told her I'd explain it all when I saw her.

We did meet for lunch and I saw her a few times after that too. Our talk seemed to comfort her tremendously and she learned that our souls really do survive death.

I also learned a lot from this experience; I just have to listen to the angels and they will gently tell me whatever I need to do. Every time I listen, things work out exactly as they should. The times when I choose not to listen are when matters don't work out in the right way.

Eventually the random messages I had been receiving began occurring more frequently. One time a woman named Halina called me to come over to sign a petition. Before hanging up the phone, I told her I would meet her by her house because I was going to be driving in her area anyway. As soon as I stepped out of my car and walked towards her house, I felt her deceased aunt's presence very strongly. At first I ignored the feeling, but then I could not anymore.

I asked her, "Who is Helen? She wants you to forgive her. She didn't mean to cause everyone all that pain by withholding her money."

Halina stood there shocked, and told me that she was very upset with her Aunt Helen who had passed away a few months earlier. Apparently her aunt had left people out of her will, and there were other problems as well concerning her aunt's money. Halina went on to tell me she couldn't find it within herself to forgive her aunt. I explained to her that her aunt would not be able to move on until she forgave her, and asked her to understand that her aunt did not know at the time how her actions had affected everyone.

This incident made me realize that when we leave our bodies, we are able to feel how we have affected others by our actions, and this includes our *good* deeds as well as those that are considered not so good. After we cross over, we actually judge ourselves and, if we feel the need to, we seek to rectify our actions.

My First Official Reading

When I first began receiving messages, my friend, Alice, called and told me that her sister-in-law, Barbara, was distraught because she had lost both her parents within a short period of time. Alice had heard about the messages I had received for Halina, so she asked me if I could possibly talk to Barbara. I explained to her that I would meet with Barbara, but I couldn't guarantee if her parents would come through with messages.

We made arrangements, and a few days later, Barbara came to my house. At that time, the only thing I knew about her was that she was Alice's sister-in-law and she had lost both of her parents. I remember being extremely nervous because this was to be my first official "reading." However, after some small talk, and realizing that Barbara was nervous as well, I was able to relax and open up to whatever I needed to hear.

I can't remember who came through first that day, but I do remember that I received *four hours* of messages from all members of Barbara's family. It seemed that everyone who had passed on in her family came through that day. The messages included specific names, details, and feelings.

When her mom first came through, she showed me Barbara looking out the window at an angel that was holding a large shell. When I asked Barbara what this meant, she told me that just before she came to my house, she was looking at her backyard through her window at a statue of a cherub pouring water into a shell. As Barbara was gazing out the window, she asked her mother to please let her know that she was all right.

I was reluctant to relay the following message I received because I thought it was insignificant. I felt as if I needed to ask Barbara to name the Seven Dwarfs. When I finally gave in and told her what I was feeling, Barbara explained to me that her mom absolutely loved Snow White and often requested that she name all Seven Dwarfs.

Her mother came through with a number of other messages as well, but the most important one was that she was sending a tremendous amount of love and peace, allowing her daughter to know that she was okay.

Barbara's father also came through, but not with as many messages as her mother did on that day. He first showed me a cardinal and said that it was him. I asked Barbara what this meant and she replied that she had seen a cardinal that morning and even wondered if it was her father saying hello. He was confirming that indeed it was. He also said that one day soon Barbara would be receiving these messages herself. Then many of her other relatives appeared and gave me their names and other details. Barbara's aunt Grace came through and mentioned her children by name: Jason, Jean, and Sharon. Then a wonderful, playful aunt named Emma came through and said to tell Rachel, her daughter, that she loved her. Then she showed me a duck that Barbara had drawn for her when Barbara was younger. Her uncle, Everett, came through and said he was worried about his children, and mentioned them all by name also—Johnny, Bucky, and Regina. Then, when a younger Everett came through, I was confused. When I asked Barbara if there was a younger Everett on the other side as well, she said Everett had a son with the same name, and he had recently crossed over.

Her relatives were so excited to come through that day, and it reminded me of the scene in the movie *Ghost* where Whoopie Goldberg screams, "One at a time, please!" Her family continued to give me messages for four hours, and then I finally needed to conclude the reading because I had to pick up my children from school.

When it was all over, Barbara felt so much better, knowing not only that both her parents were okay, but so were all her other relatives. I was very surprised by the whole thing, and couldn't believe I was able to receive so much information, including names and details from those who had crossed over.

It was that night when I first knew without a doubt that we do not just die. The soul indeed goes on, and I rationalized that since all of Barbara's deceased relatives were all okay, so were mine and everyone else's.

Even my prayers were different that evening. Before that day, I would pray that the loved ones in my life who had crossed over were at peace. Now I thanked God, *knowing* they were at peace. What a difference!

Since that first reading, whenever Barbara is upset or there is something she needs to know from the other side, her mother comes through loud and clear. One night, her mother appeared in my bedroom doorway, telling me to call Barbara right away. Because it was in the middle of the night, I did not do so immediately, but instead waited until the next day. When I talked to Barbara the following day, I described to her what her mother was wearing and even her hairstyle. Barbara told me her mother had never worn her hair that way and went to get some photographs to show me what her mother had actually looked like. When she found her wedding pictures, she gasped because her mother had on the same dress and her hair was parted on the side, just as I had just described it to Barbara.

Another time, her mother had told me to go over Barbara's house right away, and since this time it was during the day, I listened. When her husband answered the door, he told me Barbara was downstairs crying because many of her mother's belongings in the basement had become damaged due to a very bad storm. When I walked in and saw Barbara, her mother immediately came and asked me to tell her not to fret over these belongings. She wanted Barbara to stop crying because material objects no longer meant anything to her.

Yet another time, Barbara's mom showed me a rose and told me to call Barbara right away. When I called and gave her the message, Barbara became very excited. Her mother had often joked about a rosebush in her yard which never bloomed and had even placed artificial roses in it as a joke. And a few days earlier, eight huge roses had bloomed in that very same rose-bush!

There are many other instances when Barbara's mother came through (and her other relatives as well), but I'll just relay one more. I was vacuuming one evening, and her mother came to tell me to go to the local Barnes and Noble bookstore immediately. She was very persistent, so I finally gave in and went. As I walked into the store, I was not at all surprised that Barbara was standing in the entranceway. She seemed perplexed as she asked me, "What are you doing here?" When I looked at her, and I put my hands on my hips and laughed, she knew that her mother had done it again.

And just as her father had predicted, Barbara now does automatic writing, which means that she is able to receive messages herself! She sits down to write and receives messages from her mother and father. Her parents are very much aware of what is going on in her life, and this is such a comfort to her. Now she is also able to spread the news that our souls really are eternal. And what a blessing that is!

I Could Now Give Readings

After all the messages I received during my first meeting with Barbara, I knew without a doubt that I was capable of giving readings. However, it took me quite a while to feel confident enough to schedule readings at my office. (During that time, I had only performed healings at my office, and if I received messages, I would relay them to clients as I was working on them.) By word of mouth, I started getting more and more clients who wanted to hear from their deceased loved ones. I don't know how or when, but I eventually decided to give in to the many requests I had, and have been doing readings ever since.

Cherel

Cherel came to me with the hope of communicating with her deceased father. I always tell clients when they come to see me that I cannot guarantee who will come through, and this was no exception. As I began talking to Cherel during this first session, a man came through whose name was Mike. Cherel said that yes, she did have a close friend named Mike, but he was still very much alive. I didn't know what to say to her because I felt him very strongly in the room with us. He gave us a few messages, but the most important one was that he was okay. He then went on his way.

Cherel left that day quite perplexed because we didn't know what to make of that reading. After all, she thought Mike was still alive, so why would he be coming to give her messages?

The next day, however, I received a phone call from Cherel, who was crying very hard. She had just found out that her friend, Mike, had indeed passed away two weeks earlier and was unable to say good-bye to her. I truly believe that Mike had pushed Cherel to come see me so that he could let her know that he had crossed over and was okay.

This incident was a very important learning experience for me too. When I started receiving messages, I was not sure how I was getting the information. Sometimes I even thought that I may have been reading the person's mind. However, this could not have been the case when I received messages from Mike, since Cherel was not even aware that he had crossed over!

Since that first reading, Cherel has been coming to see me regularly, sometimes bringing her children and husband with her. Other friends and relatives come through as well, but it was Mike who came through again one day when Cherel brought her daughter, Jessica, to my office. Mike brought up a few things, including that Jessica had been Tiger Lily in a school play and that he had taken her to a restaurant called Fuddruckers. Jessica was embarrassed, however, when I told her that Mike was showing me lipstick. When I asked Jessica what it meant, her face turned bright red, and she confessed to her mother who had been in the room with us that she had taken her mother's lipstick from her purse earlier that day. She then gave her mother a hug and said that she was very sorry.

Since then, Mike has come through on a number of different occasions. He always wants Cherel to know that he's okay and is with her and her family. His soul truly lives on!

Denise

Denise had come to see me a few times, but it is the reading that I gave her on her birthday that stands out the most in my mind. She came in that day saying that she would do anything just to see her deceased father one more time. Since I had received messages from her father every time she came, I knew he was listening to her request. I told her to ask out loud for her father to appear to her and expect him to respond.

She asked, "Daddy, I want to see you one more time, please."

Within minutes, both of us saw a swirling circle of light which looked like it was dancing on the car parked outside my office. We were both staring at it, mesmerized, when it entered through the window and came into my office. It was *gorgeous*, with swirls of various colors, spinning around and around. Then we both saw a shadow of a man and a little girl holding hands, coming out of the light, walking away in the distance. Her father was giving us a magnificent glimpse of Denise and him many years earlier.

This had been the first time that a client of mine was able to experience exactly what I was experiencing. This whole incident went on for more than an hour, and finally, Denise had to leave to go back to work.

Her father stayed with me even after Denise left and when I was in the car driving home. He had told me to turn to a specific radio station, and when the song came on, he wanted me to tell her that it was his song for her. I then called to tell her about the song, and she began to cry.

It was truly a remarkable experience for both Denise and me. I only wish that everyone who comes into my office could also catch a glimpse of their loved ones when they come through and feel the incredible peace and love coming from them as well. Most of the time, however, I just have to relay the messages I receive to my clients, allowing them to know their loved ones are indeed okay.

Rosemarie

When my youngest son, Timmy, was in third grade and I was assisting in his classroom, I began to receive messages for his teacher, Ms. Rovegno, from her brother. Because I didn't want her to think I was crazy, and because my son was in her class, I tried to act like a "normal" person and ignore these messages. However, when I was standing next to Ms. Rovegno, I saw her brother who was in spirit form hit her over the head with a doll with yellow yarn hair. Finally, I couldn't ignore these promptings any more.

I reluctantly asked her, "Ms. Rovegno, do you believe in life after death?"

"I sure do!" she replied. "I've been trying to connect with my deceased brother, Joseph."

"But of course," I thought. "That is why he won't give up until I tell her he's here!"

I then told my son's teacher about the psychic experiences I had been having, and explained to her that her brother was behind her, hitting her over the head with a doll with yarn hair.

"That's Sleepy Head! He used to hit me over the head with her when I was young," she exclaimed, thrilled to know that he was there.

I received more messages that day in the classroom from Joseph, but even after relaying these messages to his sister, I felt that he was not yet finished. Ms. Rovegno (Rosemarie) gave me her phone number just in case her brother came again, and indeed, he returned later that night with more messages.

Whenever I stopped by her room to talk to her, Joseph often came through. It was later on in that year that I finally understood why her brother was always nearby. During the year my son was in her class, Rosemarie's father had become very ill and eventually passed away the following summer. So it was no surprise that when Rosemarie called to tell me her father had passed away a day earlier, her father made a grand entrance in my kitchen.

I was amazed that he came through so quickly, and said to her, "Oh my God, your dad is already here. He is bringing so much love and feels wonderful."

Then I paused. "Rosemarie, I don't understand this, but he is showing me a wicker basket," I added.

Although she had been previously crying, she stopped to laugh. "That's him! I just came back from the florist where I told the owner that I did not want a funeral arrangement. I asked for a certain wicker basket that I could keep, filled with beautiful flowers. He's showing you that wicker basket!"

I felt her father then say, "Tell your mother to be nice to Angelo."

She laughed, "My mother and Angelo were having a disagreement as to whether or not to keep my father's casket open or shut at the wake. My mom was a little tough on Angelo. I'll tell her to behave herself!"

Since my son was in her class, I became very close to Rosemarie. She is such a pleasure to be around and I hope we never lose touch with each other. Not only is she one of the best teacher's my son has ever had, she's also a wonderful person and friend. I thank her brother for bringing the two of us together.

As I have learned many times, there are no coincidences. I was just finishing writing about Rosemarie when I started to get a strong feeling that I needed to call her. I wasn't sure if I was writing about her because I was getting these feelings, or I was getting these feelings because I was writing about her and bringing her energy to me. In any case, I ignored these inner promptings for three days, but could not any more. I did not talk to Rosemarie in a long time, so she was surprised when I called her.

"Ro, this is Karen." I said. "I have that feeling again, just like when your brother was around me. I've felt this way for three days now, but didn't call you until now. Are you okay?"

"Hi!" she said, then sounded very sad and added, "How's my angel mom?" (She used to call me that when my son was in her class.)

"I'm fine," I replied, "but what is going on with *you?*"

Her voice cracked. "On Monday, I found out that Country died!" (During the time I was receiving messages from her brother, the name Country came up a few times. Country was the nickname of Rosemarie's old boyfriend, Gary, whom she had admitted was the only man she had ever really loved. One time Rosemarie and I were driving home from a baseball game when someone came through and showed me a huge cowboy hat. We didn't understand what it meant at the time.)

"And the worst part," she added, "is that he died five years ago, and I did not find out until now!"

I could hear it in her voice that she was having a very hard time with this news. I talked to her for awhile, and then hung up the phone. After a few minutes, I remembered that the messages I had received a few years ago when my son was in her class were about Country, but we discounted them, thinking that her brother was just acknowledging that she used to go out with Country. It then dawned on me that Country had already been on the other side at that time and was trying to inform Rosemarie that he was in spirit form and was okay. (I wonder why we didn't listen to him back then. I think it was because he was only forty-seven at the time, and we did not want to believe that he could have died at such a young age.)

I called Rosemarie back a few hours later, after feeling Country around me that night. I didn't want to bother her, but knew I had to talk to her again. After a brief hello, I had to come right to the point.

"I keep seeing stars. Then I see an open window," I explained to her. "Do these things mean anything to you?"

At first they did not, but as we began to talk again, she stated, "I remember something now about when I was in the Rockies and I went camping with Country. As we looked up at the stars in the sky, I told him that the sky was Heaven's Cathedral."

I felt a tug on my shoulder and goose bumps appeared over my entire body. I then realized what he was trying to tell Rosemarie. "He's saying that he is in Heaven's Cathedral now, and he's just fine. Please understand that."

She started to cry. After we talked a little more, she figured out what the open window had meant. "He would always say that an open window was God's way of giving us a new opportunity," she said.

I replied, "This must be Country's way of saying that he was in a world now with many new opportunities. He wants you to know that he's okay. Please do not be sad for him."

Of course this story does not end here. Needless to say, Rosemarie feels so much better now knowing that the man she had always loved is still around her. She, of course, is dealing with the pain of knowing that she will not be together physically with him again in this life, but she believes they will indeed be joined again in the next. Their love for each other was too strong for it to be any other way!

CHAPTER 2

Experiences before the Light

Life is a succession of lessons which must be lived to be understood.

—Ralph Waldo Emerson

When I'm asked if I was always psychic, I answer quite simply that I had limited psychic abilities when I was younger. My father used to take me to the racetrack with him to bet on the horses because he said I was lucky. As I look back, I realize I was the luckiest when I had nothing else on my mind to worry me— no tests, no homework, and no family problems. This would all make sense later on in my life. I had no idea at the time that these distractions were interfering with my being able to "pick up" on things.

As I look back, there were a number of "coincidences" that occurred when I was younger. I remember a dream that I had in high school of going to my locker and finding it taped shut. When I opened up the locker, I found a huge stash of sanitary napkins inside. It was a quite a vivid dream! Anyway, the next morning when I had gone to school and walked to my locker, I was not at all surprised at what I saw. My locker was all taped up, and after spending some time trying to peel off all that tape, when I opened the locker, various brands of sanitary napkins came tumbling out onto the floor. (We had a class clown who

16

thought this was very funny.) Because I had a preview of this in my dream, I just rolled my eyes and threw everything out.

Still another so called "coincidence" occurred in my teen years. When I was in eighth grade, my friend and I were making prank phone calls (yes, I'm sorry to say I did that), and I randomly dialed seven numbers. My friend and I were being silly, and when some boy answered, we started to talk to him. We asked him where he lived, and he told us the name of a nearby town. Then, after talking to him for quite a long time, he said he was going to put his friend on the phone. When his friend picked up the phone, and told us his name, I almost fainted! It was the boy that I liked at that time. He happened to be visiting this boy who I didn't even know, and without even knowing how or what I had done, I was able to find him by dialing a random number. At that time, I thought it was just an incredible coincidence.

I also recall when I was in college and my husband (who was my boyfriend at the time) was going to take the LSATs which is a test to get into law school. He was worried about what he was going to get on it, and I said, "Don't worry because you're going to get a 720 (which was very good). He poo-pooed me, rolled his eyes and said, "Yeah right, I wish."

He ended up going to visit his grandfather in Italy during the time he was expecting to receive his test results in the mail. He asked me to go to his house every day to see if the letter with his score results had arrived, and to call him up as soon as it did. On the day when it did come, I called him up and told him what he had received—a 721! (Okay, so it was one number off.) He thought I was making it up, and couldn't wait to get home so that he could see for himself what he had received. When he came home, he knew I was telling the truth, and to this day, 721 is still his "lucky number."

When I was younger, I did have an inner knowingness about what was going to happen before it did, and I often knew how genuine a person was by looking into his or her eyes. However, all these things were really nothing compared to what I was going to experience after my experience with the light.

I often wonder if my actions as a child prepared me for what I was going to do when I got older. Comparing myself to other children at the time, I realized I was very different. I used to read the Bible and go into my room and say the rosary every day. I also walked to the local church by myself often, and tried to attend mass during the week, especially during Holy Week. I didn't tell anyone about what I was doing; I just did it. However, when I look back now, I realize during that time I was very religious, whereas now I consider myself very spiritual. Now I realize that religion divides people into groups, whereas *spirituality* unites them. At that time, religion gave me a deep sense of peace, but not the sense of peace that I experience today. Back then I believed in God, but now I *know* God. Yet, I was extremely close to God, even back then. I always had God in mind throughout all my younger years, as well as my older years. And the more I felt my connection to God, the more my psychic awareness increased.

In the beginning, when my psychic abilities began to expand, however, I sometimes picked up on information that I did not want to know. This especially was the case when I had a certain precognitive dream (seeing the future in a dream) of my cousin Lora. In the dream, Lora, who was only in her thirties at the time, died when her house was engulfed in flames. When I awoke from that dream, I was terrified because I knew that this dream was different; it felt real. When I called up Lora to make sure that she had no fire hazards in her house, she assured me that she did not. However, a few months later, she was diagnosed with colon cancer and later passed away from the disease.

The events in that dream were in fact just symbols of everything that was about to occur. The house that was on fire was actually her body that was being destroyed by the cancer.

I often wonder if I could have prevented her passing if I had somehow figured out what the dream had meant right away. However, from all that I have learned since then, I truly believe it was her time to leave her body and go home to heaven. As difficult as it is, I have to accept this.

In the middle of one night during the same time that my cousin was dying, I woke up and somehow just *knew* that someone was ready to leave his or her body. I felt so much confusion going on around the spirit and it was very frightened. About an hour later, I sensed that it left its body, and with that, it shared with me the most incredible peace that it was experiencing. (Now remember, this was before I was able to feel and receive messages from spirits.) With this wonderful sense of peace, I knew that it was trying to tell me that it was okay. Not only was it okay, it was in "heaven." I assumed it was Lora who had died and had come to tell me she was all right.

When the phone rang about 5 AM the next morning, before I heard who was on the phone, I said, "Yes I know." It was my sister, Nora, on the other end of the line, and she had called to tell me that my Uncle Phil had passed away during the night, not my cousin Lora. I had the wrong person, but I had sensed his whole passing and knew that my Uncle Phil was at peace. From that point on, I began to read every book I could about near-death experiences, so that I could learn more about what I had experienced that night.

At this point in my life, it seemed that most of my psychic experiences occurred when I was falling asleep. One of these instances occurred when I first moved into my second house and was lying down, ready to doze off. For some reason, I felt I should open my eyes; it was then that I saw a transparent man staring down at me in bed. It seemed as if he were wondering what I was doing in that room. I must admit I was scared because I didn't understand who he was or why he was there. I later found out that the previous owner had died from a heart attack in the house.

Another time when I was about to fall asleep after reading *A Course in Miracles*, I felt a strong presence near me. When I looked up, I saw the spirits of two adorable little black children looking down at my book. At that time, seeing this sort of thing was not a usual occurrence for me, and again, I was afraid. As soon as I experienced fear, the vision of these children immediately left me.

Within a month or so of that incident, when I was ready to fall asleep, I felt myself leaving my body though my crown chakra (the top of my head). I didn't realize yet that we leave our bodies when we fall asleep and I thought I was dying. Just as I felt myself leaving, I thought of my young children and thought, "I can't, I can't, I can't." I immediately jolted right back into my crown chakra and my whole body shook. It was then that I realized I had control of whether or not I left, and I was no longer frightened.

Throughout those years of embracing my psychic abilities, I was also raising my three children. During that time I read every book I could find about angels, near-death experiences, alternative healing, and so forth, and learned all I possibly could in this way.

Then I started to meditate, and that's when things really began to happen. While praying is *talking* to God, I learned that meditating was *listening* to Him. Through meditation I was able to quiet myself and listen to God within me. When I was just beginning to learn how to meditate, I used a guided meditation tape so that my mind wouldn't wander; eventually I learned how to meditate by listening to soothing music which helped me to relax and quiet my mind. I began to feel better, calmer, and as a wonderful by-product, my intuitive abilities increased.

During that time, I saw an ad in a local New Age newspaper about a type of healing which interested me called Ro Hun Therapy. In this type of therapy, which was developed by Patricia Hayes, it is recognized that feelings actually exist as energies held within our chakras (I'll explain more about chakras in a later chapter) and in the aura. The Ro Hun therapist helps the person to release negative energies stored in these areas. I booked an appointment with a therapist named Jay, and it went very well; then I scheduled another one. However at the next appointment, Jay tried something on me that he had just learned. He told me to breathe in through my first chakra, and as I was inhaling, imagine my breath spinning and weaving around my spine clockwise, rising through each chakra. When it finally reached the top, I was supposed to breathe it out of my third eye and crown chakras. He told me to do this breathing exercise three times.

When I finished the third round of breaths, all of a sudden, I felt a surge of energy rising and pulsating from my feet, then traveling all the way up my body and out of my head. This rising energy lasted for several hours. Jay told me that this had never happened before to any of his other clients. He said my kundalini energy was rising, which usually was a very good thing. He knew, however, that if kundalini energy rose too quickly within a person, he or she could go insane. Therefore, after the appointment, he took me directly to a local bookstore so that I would be able to read about kundalini energy and see exactly what was happening to me.

What I found out was that kundalini is the spiritual energy that lies dormant in every person, and it is coiled like a snake at the base of the spine. When it is awakened, which usually happens after many years meditation, it rises up the spine and awakens our psychic abilities and increases our spiritual knowledge. Although I didn't realize this at first, after the kundalini energy rose in me, all these abilities were awakened in me so quickly that I couldn't keep up with what was happening! As the days, weeks, and months went by, I was able to understand more fully how to use these abilities to help others in their daily lives. At first I was afraid to share with people the messages I was receiving, but then I simply couldn't ignore these messages any longer. I was being shown everything for a reason, and in the majority of the cases, the messages were very important to those I told.

This kundalini experience occurred right before my experience with the light. I believe it opened me up so I was able to hear and feel what was about to happen that would change my life forever. I am not advising you to force your kundalini energy to rise as quickly as it did for me. I would, however, recommend you to begin to meditate every day. This in itself will allow your energy to slowly rise at the rate that is correct for you. (See Chapter on How to Communicate with Angels and Deceased Loved Ones for more details on how to meditate.) After you meditate for a while, you will gain inner peace, and your psychic abilities should increase dramatically. All you need to do is be patient and just allow it to happen.

You can see it really was an ongoing series of events that took me to where I'm at now in understanding and using my psychic abilities. Each consecutive event came exactly when I was ready for it and not before. (And so it will be for you.) As will be shown in subsequent chapters, many synchronicities are still happening now. At this point in my life, I'm ready for anything and can't wait to see what's going to happen next!

CHAPTER 3

Fitting in with Those Who Do Not Understand

Do not go where the path may lead, go instead where there is no path and leave a trail.

—Ralph Waldo Emerson

It definitely has not been easy trying to keep all these things I know inside. In the past, I tried to fit in with everyone else so I didn't seem strange. Only during the last few years have I finally been able to "come out of the spiritual closet." Even now, though, many who have known me for years are still not even aware of what I am able to do! I just share my inner knowingness with those who I feel are ready to hear and will understand what I'm about to share. If they are interested or ask me questions, then I can't stop talking about what I know. After all, when I speak of my experiences, I am free to be who I really am! However, if I feel someone doesn't understand or is not interested, I never force anything on him or her or even bring such things up.

One of my old friends, Stephanie, attended my first angel seminar, and when it was over, she came up to me and told me how she couldn't believe that it was me speaking that day. After all, I used to be very shy and withdrawn. Now I was up there speaking to a room full of people about angels. Yes, that was so true, but now I couldn't keep it in anymore. But the fact was that not only was I willing to finally share this message, but Stephanie was also now ready to hear it.

She asked me how I decided to do angel seminars because I've always been extremely frightened of going up in front of the room to speak. I reminded her that a few years earlier, I had worked as a substitute teacher at the local elementary school. This gave me the opportunity to speak in front of a group of children. Because I love children so much, I wasn't nervous at all; it actually was a lot of fun.

Then one day I took my friend, Crystal, out to lunch for her birthday to a local hotel's restaurant. After we were done eating, and we were walking down the corridor to go home, I felt a hand on my cheek, pushing my head to look at an empty conference room. As I glanced inside, I did a double take! I *saw* myself behind a podium, speaking to a group of people. I knew right away I had to go into the office to get information and available dates, and within a few days, I booked the room for my first angel workshop.

Since that time, I've done a number of angel seminars, and the angels always see to it that the right people attend. There was one time though, when a couple of people came to one of my seminars who did not understand. The energy in the room did not feel right throughout the whole day, so from that time on, I always pray that only those who are supposed to be there are. And that has worked ever since!

Now I no longer need to "fit in." I am proud of who I am and what I do. I'm willing to talk about my experiences at all times and help people in any way I can by answering questions they may have or by teaching them. (Most people come to me when *they* are ready.) As stated before, I would never force my convictions on anyone, nor do I try to persuade anyone to change his or her beliefs. I always tell others to look within themselves to see what feels right to them. If they are unsure, they should meditate and pray about anything they need to know, and they will always get their answer.

The more I have come out of the spiritual closet, the more I have surrounded myself with spiritually minded people. I have since opened a metaphysical and holistic center with coworkers of like minds and have been very happy ever since because I am now able to truly be myself. Most of my clients have found me simply by word of mouth. With all this said and done, I have learned a very powerful lesson which I would like to pass on to you. Please be yourself and be open to share your gifts with all those who are interested in what you have to offer. (Remember, though, never force your ideas on anyone.) People will find *you*. It is really funny how the universe works in joining people with similar energies. Only by being yourself will you find true peace within. And by finding the peace within yourself, you will be able to extend this peace to others as well!

CHAPTER 4

Loved Ones Setting up Events So They Can Give Messages

With a definite, step-by-step plan—ah, what a difference it makes! You cannot fail, because each step carries you along to the next, like a track...

—Scott Reed

Loved ones who have crossed over sometimes set up a series of events so they are able to come through to their family and friends. On occasion these events are so detailed and carefully thought out that it shocks everyone involved as to how they managed to make everything happen. The story of how Sue's husband, Paul, set up events so he would be able to come through is a perfect example of this.

Paul's Perfect Plan

As mentioned in the previous chapter, I used to be a substitute teacher for the local elementary school and preschool. I then began practicing healing and doing angel work, so I didn't have the time to teach any more, and told both schools to take me off their list.

However, even though I hadn't subbed for more than two years, I received a phone call from a woman from the preschool, asking me if I could assist another teacher on a class trip the following week. I told them I could not go, but if they truly were desperate and couldn't find anyone else, I would rearrange my schedule and come in for them. A few days later I received another phone call, asking if I could sub because, although they had asked eight people, none of them were able to come in on the specific day of the class trip. Hearing this, I gave in and told them I would be there.

When I went in for the class trip, I felt out of place because many of the teachers who used to work there that I had known were gone. However, as we were waiting for all the children to arrive, I was surprised when I looked up and saw the familiar smiling face of Sue. She was a wonderful strong woman who had lost her husband, Paul, in the World Trade Center on September 11th. I had seen Sue a few times in my office, and her husband always came through loud and clear. Although she hadn't visited me in a while, she had just called a week earlier to arrange for her two young children to meet me the following Monday.

"What are you doing here?" she asked, as we gave each other a big hug. "My daughter, Daria, is in the other class and she's going on the class trip."

"Really? That's wonderful!" I told her they were desperate for a substitute for the class I was in and we were also going on the class trip. "Show me which one is your daughter, and I'll keep an eye on her to make sure she's okay," I added.

She walked me over to the other classroom and pointed out her adorable daughter to me. Then the teacher I was assisting asked me to come back and help her, so I had to leave Sue to go back to the class I was assisting. I said good-bye to her and she left.

The children from the two classes climbed onto the school bus, and we eventually arrived at a local farm to pick pumpkins and go on hay rides because it was Halloween. The children from my class climbed into the tractor which consisted of two long, hay-filled rows facing each other. When it came time for me to sit down, there was no room!

The woman who worked on the farm asked me to go on the other tractor. I thought it was quite a coincidence that Daria was on that vehicle and started to wonder if Paul had something to do with all this. I began to talk to Daria, and we laughed and were able to get to know one another. We climbed off the tractor, and I joined my class to pick pumpkins and enjoy the animals and Halloween decorations.

When it was time to go back, again, there was no room on the hayride with my class, so I had to sit on the tractor with the other class where Daria was. Again, I was able to speak to her and I told her I knew her mommy, and she was going to come see me the following Monday. She said she knew who I was because her mommy already told her about me. (Sue had told her that I was the angel lady who was able to talk to her daddy.) We talked and laughed together until we climbed off the hayride.

Again, I joined my class, and all the children from the two classes climbed into the school bus. I helped the children buckle up their seat belts, and when I was finished, the only available seat on the bus was all the way in the back. At this point, I was not at all surprised at who was sitting next to the empty seat— Daria! I sat down next to her, and we both smiled at each other. We talked a little and then I felt her dad, Paul, right next to us. He was showing me that Daria had caught a fish. Because I did not want to frighten her, I did not say her daddy was with us. I did, however, ask her if she had ever caught a fish.

She replied, "Yes, I caught a fish in the summer! Everyone was crabbing, but I caught a fish. It was a nice fish."

Her father was telling me that he was with her when she caught it. Then he told me her birthday, April 3, and her sister's birthday, August 15, as well. I asked Daria if these birthdays were correct, and she said yes. Tears started trinkling down my face;

this was amazing! Again, I didn't want her to become frightened, so I didn't tell her that her daddy was there. I waited until I saw her mom, Sue, to verify all these things and tell her that Paul came on the class trip with us.

We arrived back at the preschool about twenty minutes before the parents were going to pick up their children. I grew very impatient waiting for Sue to arrive. I tried calling her at home, but she was not there. It seemed like eternity, but she finally pulled into the parking lot, and I ran after her car. She opened the window and I whispered to her that Paul came on the class trip with us. She was on her cell phone, and I felt Paul was anxious and couldn't wait any longer. I knew that he wanted her to hang up immediately.

Finally she hung up the phone, and I was able to tell her the whole thing—how everything was arranged—how eight people turned down coming in that day to sub, how I didn't sub in two years, but did that day, how I had to sit with Daria's class because there was no room for me on the other tractor, how Daria had no partner on the bus ride home, and how I sat next to her a second time. Sue confirmed that Daria did catch a fish during the summer, Daria's birthday indeed was April 3, and her sister's was August 15. All I can say is that Paul wanted his children to know that he was okay and was with them, and had somehow arranged for everything to happen so that he would be able to come through for them. I don't know how he was able to do all this. All I can say is that he is a truly amazing, determined soul who wanted his family to know he was still watching over them!

Loved ones who have crossed over, especially those who have left suddenly, often remain around their family and friends to guide and protect them. When they try to give messages to those still here and these messages aren't being heard, they find any avenue they can to demonstrate they are still around. Sometimes they set up all different kinds of scenarios to arrange for a medium like myself to be near their loved ones to relay

messages for them. Paul's setting up all the events at the Halloween hayride was a perfect example of this. Since he could not
pick up the phone to call his family, he used me as his communication device.

And just when I thought Paul was finished with setting up
events, he did it again! I hope you can follow this next story
because this one truly gets complicated.

There is a local New Age bookstore that has weekly Sunday
services which include healings and "messages." Throughout
the years, many people had tried to persuade me to go to one of
these services, but I had never gone. Finally one day I felt
compelled to attend, and I asked my daughter to come with me.
The service was wonderful! In the beginning, people went to the
front of the room where various healers performed "hands-on"
healing on them. We sang beautiful songs, including my
daughter's favorite, "I Hope You Dance." At the end, the
minister even had a message for *me* which was a pleasant
surprise. (I'm so used to giving messages to everyone else, but no
one ever gets them for me. The minister said there was a woman
there named Mitzi who had an Italian restaurant. This happened
to be my deceased aunt. Also, my friend, Stormy came through.
The minister said Stormy was a very strong person [that's for
sure!], and that she loved cats [very true].)

Anyway, during the whole service, I felt the deceased wife of
a gentleman who was sitting directly in front of me trying very
hard to come through. I didn't want to bother the man, so I tried
hard to ignore her signs. After the services, my daughter and I
were looking for some books in the bookstore and the man's wife
came around again. I mentioned it to my daughter and she told
me that I had to tell the man. After all, he was in this bookstore
and must have been very open to receiving messages. To make
a long story short, I finally gave in and told him the messages, and
he was happy I did. (At first, his wife said the name Dave, and
when I asked him who that was, he said, "That would be me!"

She then told me the name Hannah Leigh, which was going to be the name of their baby if they had a girl. She also said to tell Carol, her mother, that she was okay. There were also a few other messages as well.) Afterwards, I finally understood why I felt so compelled to go to that service. His beautiful wife must have been urging me to go because I found out that in three days it was going to be the year anniversary that she had passed away. Although I did not understand why, I had an inner knowing this was not going to be the last time I was going to be receiving messages from Dave's wife.

A few weeks later, I was giving a meditation class which Sue (Paul's wife) attended. I didn't understand why, but I felt that I *had* to tell her the story about Dave. When I did, she gasped. She told me that a psychic had told her to be prepared because she was going to meet a man named Dave. Wow, I thought, what a coincidence!

Sue emailed me that night and told me in the weeks before the class, she had kept running into a woman, Karen, from her town. Karen and she had both been told by others that Karen's brother-in-law and Sue should meet. That afternoon, when Sue was picking up her daughter from school, she saw Karen, and they walked up the path together. They talked about the weather, school, the kids, and other things, and then Sue asked Karen how her brother-in-law was doing. Karen said that he was still having a hard time, but he had found great comfort at a service that he went to every Sunday at a New Age bookstore. The minute Karen said that, Sue said she nearly fell over. She asked Karen if her brother-in-law's name was Dave. The woman said yes! Sue was shocked. It was the *same* Dave!

To make a long story short, both Dave's wife and Sue's husband kept trying to get the two of them together, and they finally obliged. Sue came to my office after she first met Dave to tell me that they got along well and had a lot in common. As of this writing, the two of them have been together a few times after that as well. They have developed a unique friendship, one that has been carefully guided by their loved ones.

The Rainbow Follows the Storm

When I began my healing work, a wonderful woman named Stormy found my name on Doreen Virtue's Angel Therapy website and emailed me to see if I could work with the angels to help her. After corresponding back and forth via email, Stormy and I finally were able to meet at my office, which at that time was in the back of a beauty salon.

Stormy couldn't walk due to a fall and severe complications from diabetes. Her one leg was shorter than the other and was severely swollen from many operations she had undergone to fix the leg. Although she was only thirty-eight years old, in order for her to move around, her husband, Steve, had to transport her in a wheelchair. Stormy and I immediately became close friends due to our similar interests, especially her strong faith in God and His angels. She came for a healing once a week and we spoke on the phone a few times each day.

After a few weeks of healings, Stormy astounded me when she got up out of her wheelchair and walked into my office. Out of all the healings I have done, this was one of the most memorable for me.

I have so many stories about Stormy, but these stories could fill up an entire book by itself—that's how amazing she was! I have just one regret, and that is I only knew her at the end of her short life. This high-spirited woman passed away only two years after I had met her. Right before her passing, she was very tired and repeatedly stated that she wanted to go back home. (This was her reference to heaven.) I told her to be careful about what she was saying because words are very powerful. She insisted that she meant it, and shortly after affirming her willingness to leave the earth, she suffered a heart attack from which she never recovered.

After she went into a coma and was pronounced clinically dead, Steve asked me to help him speak to the hospital board because he wanted to take her off the respirator. The hospital board finally granted its permission to unplug her from the respirator and allowed Steve to bring her home. However, before they were able to carry this all out, Stormy passed away peacefully in the hospital.

Before the heart attack, Stormy told me that she would let me know that she was okay after she crossed over, so it didn't surprise me at all at what happened the very same morning of her passing. An hour after she had died, as I was coming home from driving my children to school, I spotted a police car in front of my house.

I got out of my car and asked the officer what was going on, to which he replied, "Lady, you have a bear on your property!"

"A WHAT?" I shouted. Then I smiled because I immediately realized the bear's appearance was Stormy's way of saying she was okay. Why she chose a bear to come, I do not know, but bears have never been on my property before, nor have they been on my property after this incident. As a matter of fact, they have never been in my town at all.

Of course Stormy did not stop with just the bear incident. She has made herself known many times to her husband. She also has been with me on a number of occasions as well. For example, after I came home from her funeral, I was very tired, and plopped down on my bed to cry and rest. As I was going through the day's events in my mind, the blinds on the sliding glass door started "dancing." I called my daughter into my room to watch, and to meet Stormy, and we both laughed. I knew without a doubt that it was Stormy, and she was telling me to cheer up because she was fine.

A few weeks later, Stormy learned how to play with electricity. Oh God, did she play with the electricity! A stereo system that is connected throughout my house would keep turning itself on in the middle of the night. I eventually had to go into the living room and unplug the whole system.

A few weeks after that, Stormy somehow figured out how to turn the stereo on just in the room that I was in. When I came home from food shopping, the radio would go on by itself. She also figured out how to broadcast certain songs. It boggles my mind to think of all that she had done. One day she played a song about being where "the blind can see." (Stormy's eyesight had been very bad at the end of her life, and she was anxious to tell me that she was able to see again.)

Also, a year after Stormy died, her mom called me just to talk. As we were discussing the signs that Stormy had been giving people, the stereo turned on by itself and was blasting so loudly that Stormy's mom said she couldn't hear me. Laughing, I told her she couldn't hear me because her daughter had turned on the music again and was saying hello.

I need to mention one more thing. At the end of Stormy's life, she no longer wanted to be called Stormy, and wanted to change her name. She finally came up with the name Rainbow. Yes, it was different, but it was a pretty name, one that fit her. At her funeral eulogy, the minister asked me why she wanted to be called Rainbow, and I told him that the rainbow follows the storm. He later incorporated that into his wonderful sermon about Stormy.

When I was writing this section about Stormy, she really outdid herself! It began when I felt her presence so strongly and decided to call her husband, Steve, to see how he was doing. He informed me that it was the anniversary of the day she had died. I believe she urged me to call Steve to let him know she was okay. After talking to Steve, I went to get my mail, still feeling Stormy so strongly right next to me.

As I opened my mailbox, I was surprised to see there was a beautifully wrapped gift inside. It just so happened that Eileen, a client of mine, had left this present for me, which was a basket of miniature angel cards with beautiful sayings on them. As I was opening the plastic that was wrapped around these angel cards, one card fell out of my hand and slowly fell to the floor. I bent down to pick it up and felt chills go up and down my spine when I read what it said—*"Guardian angel, help me remember: The rainbow follows the storm."*

Stormy had done it again! I still have this magnificent angel card in a frame sitting on my desk at my office as a constant reminder to myself and everyone who comes through my door that the soul truly survives physical death and the rainbow really does follow the storm!

Stormy was a very strong personality when she was here on earth, so it was no surprise that even after her soul left her body, she set up these amazing events to prove to her friends and loved ones that she was okay. She was an actress in her living years, and she continues to give "command performances" now that she has crossed over to the other side.

I thought I had finished writing this chapter and put away my laptop. I signed onto my other computer to check my emails and received one from my friend Mary Therese. It was one of those "pass it along" letters, and it began with, *"Everything I need to know about life, I learned from Noah's Ark."* It ended with *"No matter the storm, when you are with God, there's always a rainbow waiting."* Stormy's true faith in God and her persistence in giving me this same message over and over is truly remarkable. I know she won't ever stop giving me signs, and I truly wouldn't want it any other way!

CHAPTER 5

The Telephone Connection

Alexander Graham Bell didn't contemplate the noncommunication of things. In order to float an idea into your reality, you must be willing to do a somersault into the inconceivable and land on your feet, contemplating what you want instead of what you don't have.

—Wayne Dyer

Sometimes when I'm on the phone, I receive messages from the loved ones of the person to whom I am speaking. It is almost as if the space between us didn't exist and the person on the other end is in the same room with me. One of these times occurred when a young man who had been murdered came through to say that he was okay when I was speaking on the phone with his dear friend and employer.

Jose

It was certainly Divine timing when a wonderful woman named Pam and I had met. She had come to my angel seminar and sat in the front row. At the end of the workshop, she approached me and said she felt as if she knew me from another lifetime. I sensed the strong connection with her as well. We talked for a while, promised that we would keep in touch with one another, and then went our separate ways.

About a week later, Pam called me, and I was totally unprepared for what she was about to say. One of her employees,

36

Jose, had been just been murdered, and she was *extremely* upset. As we were talking, I immediately felt Jose's presence very strongly. I told Pam that he was already coming through and surprisingly, he felt very peaceful.

The first thing he said was the name *Rosa* and with that, again, he allowed me to feel an incredible peace. Pam immediately acknowledged that his wife's name was Rosa. Next, Jose wanted Pam to ask Rosa to take good care of the cat. Afterwards, he said the word "bendito," but neither Pam nor I knew what that word meant. I asked Pam to relay all the messages to Jose's wife, including the strange word, and told her to get back to me.

Pam called me back the next day to say that Jose's wife was relieved when she heard the messages. She began crying when Pam told her Jose said "bendito" because this is the word her relatives use when someone has gone to heaven. The cat message was very relevant too because Jose had a cat he loved very much. The most important message though, was the incredible peace he relayed to me.

As Pam was talking about her conversation with Rosa, I felt Jose again, but this time he showed me a huge rock. When I asked Pam what this meant, she laughed and said she was looking out her window at a very huge rock. Mentioning this rock was Jose's way of validating that he was also with Pam at that time. Pam and I eventually ended our telephone conversation and promised that we would get together soon.

Pam's sister-in-law, Rose, invited me over for lunch shortly after Jose had been murdered. As I was sitting in Rose's kitchen, I suddenly began shivering uncontrollably and just couldn't get warm. I had to put on my coat, and Rose covered me with a blanket. I told Rose to call Pam because I felt Jose in the room. She tried to call Pam, but she was not answering the phone. Finally, Pam picked up the phone, and apologized to Rose, "I'm sorry it took so long to come on, but I was in the freezer." (She owns a food catering business.)

When Rose relayed this message to me, I asked for the phone so I could speak directly to her. I then told Pam what had just happened, and she laughed and said she was wearing Jose's coat when she was in the freezer. We then understood what Jose was trying to say. He was telling Pam that he had been with her the whole time and he was okay.

About a month later, Pam and I went to a class together that was being held at a hotel near Pam's home. I rode in the car with Pam, and as we were passing a certain shop, I began to feel Jose very strongly again. (At the time, I didn't know the shop was Pam's catering place where Jose had worked with her.) He began flashing pictures in front of me to show me what had happened to him. He was drinking beer in a bar, arguing with a man. A man hit him over the head with a pool cue and then stabbed him in the chest. (Pam did already tell me that he was stabbed, but didn't tell me he was hit over the head.) After I relayed this to Pam, she explained that when she was shown Jose's body after he was murdered, she had felt his head and there *was* a huge bump on it, and he *was* killed in a bar.

Right after Jose showed me the murder scene, he immediately allowed me to experience his complete serenity. I certainly do not understand it, but even after being murdered, Jose was definitely at peace. This was the same peace he had allowed me to experience a month earlier when he had just been murdered.

I truly believe that Pam was guided to come to my angel seminar right before Jose was about to be murdered because she was going to need the connection with me to receive messages from her dear friend and employee who was going to die only a week later. Immediately after he was murdered, he wanted his loved ones to know that he was okay, so he first came through when I was on the phone with Pam. He continued to give messages after that day, but these initial messages were the most important of all.

Madeline

It was around 8 PM, and my friend, Marion, and I were on the phone discussing carpooling for the next day. After we started to talk, I felt someone with me from the spirit world. At that instant, Marion went on to say that her friend's mother, Madeline, had passed away at 4 PM that day. It was then that I felt a tap on my shoulder, and I realized it was Madeline making herself known to me.

"Marion," I said. "She's here; Madeline's already here!"

"I knew it!" she exclaimed. "We told her to come to you after she crossed over so we would know she was okay."

Madeline came through with messages for about an hour. Finally it was time to drive my daughter to her dance class, so I had to hang up the phone, even though I knew that Madeline was not yet finished. I apologized to Marion, but told her I'd call her back.

I dropped off my daughter at her dance class, and then all of a sudden, the aroma of incense that is used during high masses in Catholic churches filled my entire car. I quickly called Marion from my cell phone.

"My car is filled with the fragrance of incense they use at high masses. Why?"

Marion laughed. "Madeline wanted a high mass for her funeral. Linda (Madeline's daughter) didn't arrange that yet at the church. I'll call her now to make sure she does!"

Madeline came through very strong that day, but she didn't stop there. Since then, whenever I see her daughter, Linda, she always gives a message to let Linda know that she is okay. And as always, just thinking of Madeline brings her around.

As I was writing this section, she came through again. She urged me to call her daughter, Linda, which I did. As Linda answered the phone, I felt a lot of commotion around her, and she had to speak very loudly in order for me to hear her. She told me she had fifty people at her house because she was hosting a birthday party for her sister-in-law. I told Linda that her mother had urged me to call her.

"I felt my mom around the house the whole time! She loved my sister-in-law, so I knew she would come to the party. Thanks so much for confirming that she really is here," Linda added. "I'm going to tell anyone at the party who will listen that my Mom really is here!"

Then about a month later, I was at a party and ran into Linda again. As soon as I saw Linda, I felt her mom. I relayed the message that I had heard. "What's with the gas?" I blurted out.

Linda started laughing. "My father had such bad gas the past few days that he couldn't even go out. My mom is telling you about my father."

I laughed and added, "She wants him to feel better. And now she's showing me bananas."

"That's funny," Linda replied. "My father has colitis and I told him not to eat fruit. He told me that he had a banana and was going to eat it anyway."

I saw Linda again the next week at our son's basketball practice. Prior to that, all day I had been hearing "Sparky," and I did not know why. I asked everyone I saw if they knew a Sparky, and they all said no. Then I gave up because I couldn't figure out what it meant.

When I saw Linda I heard the name "Hank" and asked who this was. She told me that she had a close friend from high school named Hank, but his real name was John Sparky. I laughed and told her about what I had been hearing all day. I then told her to call John to see if he was okay.

Linda called me a week later to tell me that she finally was able to get in touch with John, and he told her that he was in tremendous pain because he was in a bad automobile accident. At that point I realized it must have been one of John's loved ones who came through the previous week with the intention of getting Linda to check up on John.

Linda later informed me that John worked at a store in the same town where I work. When she explained where it was, I told her I didn't know that area, but maybe one day I would stop by there to see how John was doing. I was not planning on finding the store as quickly as I did though! The *very next day* I had to make copies of a flyer I was putting out for a class I was going to be teaching. The shop where I normally make copies was closed, so instead, I went to a place I'd never been to before. The man who made the copies told me to come back in ten minutes, so I decided to take a walk outside to waste some time. To my surprise, the store where John worked was only a few feet away from where I was! I went inside and asked the manager if a man named John Sparky worked there, and he said yes, but he was not in on that particular day. I do know, however, that whoever was pushing me to see him will make sure I go back at a different time when he *will* be in.

To this day, I believe it was Madeline who had helped to bring John's loved one through. Madeline is very strong-willed and is probably telling those on the other side that she knows a woman (me) who could relay messages to their family members who are still here. I suspect there are others who will come through to me because of Madeline, and I will be happy to oblige in any way I can to help them.

I didn't think I'd hear from Madeline again so soon, but I was wrong. A few weeks later, as I was sitting at home, I felt Linda's mom urging me to call Linda immediately. I did, but her son answered and told me that she would call me right back. Ten minutes went by and Linda still did not return the call. Madeline's mom would not leave and told me to call Linda again, so, reluctantly, I did. When Linda finally came to the phone, I asked her what was going on that her mother needed to talk to her right away. She said her husband had just been talking about the possibility of putting Linda's father in a nursing home so that he would be safe and nurtured. Linda disagreed and told her husband she was not going to allow that to happen because her mother would not have approved. When Linda was explaining this to me, I saw her mother's arms reaching out to hug her daughter. Madeline was thanking Linda for respecting her wishes by not putting her father in a nursing home.

I'm sure this will not be the last time I hear from Madeline. When she has a message she wants me to relay to her daughter, Madeline wants me to give it as quickly as possible. Even when I am not physically in the same location as Linda, Madeline will still come to me because she knows I can just pick up the phone and call her daughter.

CHAPTER 6

Off Days

Don't try to force anything.
Let life be a deep let-go.
See God opening millions of flowers every day
without forcing the buds.

—Bhagwan Shree Rajneesh, *Dying for the Enlightenment*

When I started receiving messages, I wanted to be 100% accurate every time and relay these messages for people whenever they wanted them. However, I have since learned that the messages come *when* the departed loved ones want to give them. I must admit though, that this can be very embarrassing to me and disappointing to someone who has been looking forward to a reading. Now I just accept the process and understand that I cannot force someone to come through, and I always explain this to my clients.

It was fine when I first started receiving messages because then I randomly informed people when these messages came. If a person wanted a reading, I would tell them I just did healings, and many times, but not always, I would receive messages for the person during the healing. It took a while before I finally had enough courage to give the readings that everyone wanted. Most of the time when a client comes, I am able to receive messages from his or her deceased loved ones. The reading is always the best if I have never met the person coming in because I have no frame of reference from him or her and there are no emotional ties involved.

However, there are occasions when no one comes through, or I am unable to receive anything from them if they are there. And whenever I try too hard, nothing happens. This occurred when my daughter's friend lost her beautiful sister, Raven, who crossed over from a car accident.

Raven

I can't put into words the extent of grief everyone felt after this beautiful young woman's life abruptly ended as the result of a tragic car accident. When I was offering condolences after Raven had just crossed over, I simply told her grieving parents that I knew Raven was okay. I didn't think they even heard me with all that was happening.

A few months later, I received a phone call from Raven's dad.

"What did you mean when you said that you knew she was okay?" he inquired.

I briefly told him what I knew of the afterlife, and he then asked if I could come over to see if I could receive messages from his daughter. Of course I obliged, but I don't remember ever feeling more nervous in my whole life. I knew the family, and it was more important than ever to get this right!

Even though I drove my daughter to their house many times, I felt as if I were in a daze, and I ended up getting lost. My hands were shaking so much, I couldn't control them. When I finally arrived, they were very happy to see me. We went upstairs to the parents' bedroom, and I did receive a few very personal messages at that time, and they were satisfied.

I also went another day, and was just as nervous. This time Raven showed me a rock and a rhinestone. I asked her father if the rock meant anything, and he told me that he always carries a rock that Raven gave him when she was younger. As for the rhinestone, at first, no one could figure out what a rhinestone could possibly mean. I then asked them to give me something of Raven's that I could hold to see if I could receive more messages from her, and they went upstairs and brought back a key chain that had many dangling charms. There was a small box connected to it on one end. I can't even remember who opened up the box, her mother or her father, but when they did, inside was the rhinestone Raven had shown me earlier! To me, this was a definite confirmation of the rhinestone she had shown me, but I know her father wanted more.

A few months later, they came to see me at my office. I was so nervous again and couldn't get a thing. Nothing. To make matters worse, I knew these wonderful people and I couldn't help them this time. I don't know if it was because I was so nervous or because Raven just wasn't there that day. I do know that everyone was disappointed, and I just felt awful.

Raven's parents went to three other mediums, two of whom are very famous. Her dad was disappointed each time because he was looking for something very specific that he had asked Raven to say if she was truly there. None of them, including me, has come up with what he wants to hear.

Many times our departed loved ones do not always say what we want to hear, but instead relay what they want to say. If we wait for a specific message, we may be very disappointed. I truly hope that Raven's dad receives the message he wants to hear soon from her so that he will know without a doubt that his daughter's soul really does live on. In this way, he will find the peace that has been missing in his life since the day he lost his beautiful daughter.

Back-to-Back Appointments with No Messages

There was another time that really stands out in my mind when I couldn't receive any messages. Two friends made back-to-back appointments with me. When the first one, Roseanne, came into my office, I already felt tense and after some time passed, I didn't receive anything. Then I asked her friend to come in, and again, nothing. I was so embarrassed, and was ready to give up on doing readings. Before going to sleep that night, I asked my angels to tell me in a dream what I should do, and if I should continue giving readings. I don't remember any dream, but I did wake up feeling so much more confident.

Alma's Reading

I had another reading scheduled the next day. This woman, Alma, had heard of me at work from Pat, a friend from my town. A few months before, I had received random messages from Pat's father. One time, I was driving Pat's son, Jason, home from school, and a picture of a dark shirt flashed in front of me. Somehow I knew that it was Jason's grandfather who was showing me this shirt, so I asked Jason if the shirt had meant anything to him. He told me that he had worn that shirt often because it had been his grandfather's. Immediately after he said that, I saw the words "black cow" flash in front of me. I asked Jason what that meant, and he told me his grandfather used to make him a drink he called a black cow.

Jason was very close to his grandfather and was extremely happy his grandfather had come through that day. After Jason's mom heard about these messages, she recommended me to her co-worker, Alma.

Right before Alma's appointment, I felt a woman's presence in my office. She kept repeating, "Rory, Rory. Tell Rory I'm okay." So when Alma came in, I asked her if she knew a Rory. She told me that two days earlier, a neighbor had died, and her son's name was Rory. I told Alma to make sure she told Rory that his mother was okay.

Alma's late brother, Giacomo, also came during the reading and showed me that he played the accordion. Her other brother,

Marco, also came through and showed me a donkey. When I first asked Alma what this meant, she didn't know, but then after a moment, she exclaimed, "Oh yes! Now I remember!" She explained that the previous week she had watched an old video of her brother. In it, he was pretending to be a donkey and was giving rides to children on his back.

I also saw someone shoving flowers in front of Alma's face. She didn't know what that meant, but later on that day, she called to tell me that her fiancé came home that night and surprised her when he shoved flowers in her face.

There were other messages as well in that reading, but the reason why I am sharing this is because I knew I was still able to give readings, and realized I should not give up. When I think of the times when nothing comes through, I remember what my daughter's S.A.T. tutor told me: "Everyone has off days, especially those in the creative professions, and that includes musicians, artists, dancers, and even psychic mediums."

I still don't understand exactly why there are times when nothing comes through. Perhaps the loved ones are doing something else at the time and are not available, or perhaps I am just having an off day. I do know, however, that when the message is supposed to come through, it does, and when that happens, I see how much comfort it brings to those who remain here.

Months after I finished this chapter, Roseanne, one of the women I mentioned earlier for whom I could not receive a message, came back to see me. I had a better feeling about her coming this time, so I was encouraged. All I can say is that I'm glad she came back!

Alice and Aunt Jemima

It actually started the night before the reading, when I was on the field watching my son play baseball. As I was sitting on the bleachers, I felt someone around me, and then the female presence told me her name was Alice. I thought the message was for George, a man who was sitting in front of me, and asked him if he knew an Alice who had crossed over. When he said he did not, I was embarrassed, but I knew what I had heard. There was someone with me named Alice—there was no doubt about that!

The next day I was scheduled to meet with Roseanne. As soon as she came in, I received a very strange message. I saw Aunt Jemima (yes, the pancake lady!) over my client's shoulders. When I told Roseanne what I was seeing, she said there really was an Aunt Jemima and she had visited her and her friend (who has since passed away) in their elementary school. Roseanne went on to say that it was a major extravaganza in her school when Aunt Jemima arrived in a helicopter. I asked her what her friend's name was, and when she said, "Alice," I knew she was the one who had been with me the night before! Now it all made sense.

Alice relayed an hour's worth of messages to her friend that day. There was one message however, that Roseanne did not understand. Alice kept showing me a handful of gray rocks, and she couldn't understand what that had meant. Then, when Roseanne was leaving, and as she was walking down the hallway out of my office, Roseanne said she had a strong feeling to walk back toward my room. Behind her was an Indian Medicine Wheel which people from my center had set up on a table to symbolize peace in the world. I still didn't understand the connection, but then Roseanne brought to my attention that the Medicine Wheel was made up of many rocks, some of which were gray. She wondered if perhaps the message had something to do with the Medicine Wheel. Then as we glanced down, a confetti angel was lying right in the middle of the Medicine Wheel which had not been there earlier! I screamed! We then realized that Alice had been trying to tell Roseanne that she was Roseanne's angel! Even though I receive messages all the time, this one truly amazed me. I gave Roseanne the angel and told her to keep it as a symbol that Alice was now her guide and was watching over her.

Why Alice had decided to come through the second time Roseanne came to see me and not the first, I do not know. I am extremely relieved though, that Roseanne did decide to come back. Again, the bottom line is that, in my experience, our loved ones come through when they want to come and not always when we want them to. It's the same as when they were alive and we invited them to visit, but they were too busy and couldn't make it on certain days. Sometimes they would pick a "rain date" and come another day that was more convenient for them. I believe this is what happened with Alice. She came when *she* was able to come and not before that.

CHAPTER 7

When I Wasn't Sure Whether or Not to Share the Messages I Received

To follow, under all circumstances, the highest promptings within you; to be always true to your divine self; to rely upon the inner Light, the inward Voice, and to pursue your purpose with a fearless and restful heart, believing that the future will yield unto you the reward of every thought and effort; knowing that the laws of the universe can never fail, and that your own will come back to you with mathematical exactitude, this is the faith and the living of faith.

—James Allen, *As a Man Thinketh*

There have been a number of times when I wasn't sure if I should relay the messages that were given to me from departed loved ones. Sometimes messages just didn't make any sense to me and other times they were just too embarrassing for me to repeat. Looking back now, I realize that the "craziest" messages were the ones that meant the most to people.

Our loved ones want us to laugh and to remember the funny things about them instead of being sad and grieving for them. So many times I've seen clients walk into my office crying and walk out laughing from a message a loved one had given them. Those who have crossed over often come through because they want to cheer up those who remain here on earth.

From all of this, I've learned that I always need to give the message I am receiving to the person for whom it is intended, whether it is funny, something that doesn't make sense to me, or even something that makes me blush. Many times, these messages not only brighten up my client's day, but even *my* day as well.

The Boxing Kangaroo and the Woman Smoking Cigars

A young woman named Jill had come to see me upon the recommendation of both her mother and her grandmother. After receiving messages from her grandfather, I saw a car floating above her head. On the side of the car, I saw what I thought couldn't possibly mean anything to her—a boxing kangaroo! I was reluctant to tell her what I had received because it seemed so strange, yet a male figure that was in the room kept pushing me to tell her what he had shown me.

I announced to Jill, "You may think I'm crazy, but there's a male presence in here and he's showing me a boxing kangaroo. Does this mean anything to you?"

She gasped and said, "Yes, that's my friend, Rob. He died in a car accident, and…" she smiled and added, "he boxed kangaroos in Australia!"

"No way!" I exclaimed and then took a deep breath. And to think, I almost didn't give her the message because I thought I was seeing things!

Rob then went on to display a huge cigar in front of Jill's face. Again I was perplexed. When I asked her what that meant, she smiled and told me that she smoked cigars.

I'm so glad I listened and relayed these messages to Jill. I know now that I always need to say exactly what I see, even if it doesn't make any sense to me. And from my experience, the crazier the message is, the greater the chance that it is very meaningful to my client.

Flip Wilson Impressions

I've also learned that the pictures I receive are often from my frame of reference, not my client's. One day, three sisters were in my office, hoping to communicate with their deceased relatives. Members of their family came through with messages, but at the end of the session, Faye, one of the sisters, was wondering why her husband did not come through. Just as she voiced her concern about her husband not giving her a message, I felt a male presence enter the room. I believed it was her husband and asked him to give me a sign that it was truly him. He relayed a number of messages, but one in particular was a bit confusing to me. A picture of Flip, the maintenance man from my office building, flashed in front of me. I didn't know what this could possibly mean to Faye, but I still asked her if the name "Flip" meant anything to her or her husband.

Faye laughed, "Yes it does! My husband used to do Flip Wilson impressions!"

All I can say is that it was a good thing I knew a man named Flip. I wonder how else Faye's husband would have relayed that message to me because I didn't know what Flip Wilson looked like. But then again, I'm sure her husband would have found another way to get this message to his wife!

Man with No Neck

One day Diane came in with her daughter, Cherie, and daughter-in-law, Laura. After Diane's husband came through with a number of messages, I saw a giraffe stretching his neck all the way up and then making it smaller again. You would think at this point I wouldn't doubt that this giraffe was significant. Yet I did doubt it because I thought it couldn't possibly mean anything to this woman. However, I relayed the message anyway, and it's a good thing I did.

"Why is your husband showing me a giraffe stretching out his neck?" I asked.

Diane laughed. "My husband had no neck. He couldn't wear turtlenecks because they wouldn't fit on his neck. When he fell down the stairs at the end of his life, they tried to put a neck brace on him, but it wouldn't even fit! He's showing me that he can make his neck as big as he wants to now!"

Before the giraffe message, Diane had been crying because she had missed her husband so much. I felt this was her husband's way of making her laugh, and I told her what I was feeling.

Diane replied, "That is my husband. He always tried to make us all laugh when we were sad. Sometimes we'd get very angry at him because we didn't feel like laughing when we were so upset. I can't believe he's still doing that!"

Diane and her family came in my office very distraught, but left laughing because they knew that this wonderful man was with them, with his sense of humor and all. His beautiful essence was still the same.

Playing in the Sewer

Another day, Mioko, a client who had been coming to see me regularly, asked me to send her mother, who lived in Japan, a distant healing. As I was looking at her mother's picture and sending her healing energy, her mother's father came through. I almost didn't relay one of the messages I received in which I saw Mioko placing a stick into filthy brown water. I eventually did however, and although I had given her a number of other messages, this was the message she appreciated the most. She laughed and told me that when she was little, she and her sister would take off the sewer plate that was located underneath the house and poke a stick through a hole to play with the dirty water. Although she and her sister were reprimanded when they did this, it was a very funny memory for her.

The Nudist Colony

I've received many strange messages, but the next one is one of my favorites. When I was giving a reading to Ken, a flashing picture of a nudist colony appeared in front of me. Being shy, I was reluctant to share this message with Ken, but eventually gave in and told him what I saw. He laughed and said he didn't understand what the message meant.

That same evening when I was making dinner, however, I received a phone call from him after he came back from making what turned out to be a very unique pizza delivery.

"You're not going to believe what happened just now," he was laughing; then he waited for me to guess.

I didn't know. "Come on, just tell me," I knew from his laughter that this was going to be a good one.

"I just came back from delivering fourteen pizzas..." he paused and made me wait, "to a nudist colony!"

I began laughing hysterically and waited for him to continue.

"Everyone at work was giggling when my boss told me where I had to go. I couldn't believe it," he told me.

He added, "When I got there, the first thing I saw was a naked old guy standing by the pool. I didn't want to look at him and tried to find someone with clothes on who could pay for the pizza. When I finally found someone, he told me to put the pizzas down by the guy by the pool. I wanted to run away."

"Then I saw a naked old woman walking down the road. As I glanced over to the other side, I saw at least fifteen other people standing around the pool with no clothes on," he said.

He continued, "It was like seeing the cast of the movie, *Cocoon*, naked. I put the pizzas down there by the pool and got the hell out of there as fast as I could."

I was fighting back tears from laughing so hard as he was telling me all this. Another crazy message had been right after all. And to think that I almost didn't tell Ken what I saw.

Parts of the Male Anatomy

I had been receiving a number of significant messages for an elderly woman when she was in my office. Then all of a sudden, in the middle of the reading, I saw a picture of testicles. No way was I going to share that with her! But the picture kept flashing in front of me. I was so embarrassed and didn't know what to do.

"Okay," I thought. "I'll get this over with quickly."

I took a deep breath and asked, "Would there be a reason why I'm being shown testicles?"

"Why, yes," she replied. "My husband has been having problems with his testicles, and I've been trying to get him to go to the doctor."

I never want to diagnose anything or scare anyone, but I just knew at that point to tell the woman that it would be a good idea if her husband made an appointment with his doctor to see what the problem was. I had to relate that message to her because I knew it was very important for her husband to seek medical assistance. I never did find out what happened, but I did know that her husband needed to get checked out.

And that wasn't the last time I was shown a part of the male anatomy in a reading. During one reading, when a deceased mother came through and gave me messages for her daughter, I saw a huge male organ in front of my client. I wondered what the heck that could possibly mean, since it was her mother who was giving the messages. Since it did not go away, I knew I had to relay what I saw to my client. When I asked what this meant to her, she turned bright red and then laughed. She told me that the night before her mother had died she was sitting next to her mother's bed with her friend having a discussion about the size of male organs. She told me that this conversation had gone on for quite a long time and did not think for a moment that her mother could have possibly heard her because her mom was in a coma! Now here her mom was coming through saying that she heard the whole thing!

So the lesson is this—if you know someone who is in a coma, do *not* say anything in her presence that you don't want her to hear. Contrary to what you believe, she *is* able to hear every word you say!

The Plunger

A distraught man named John came for a session to see if he could contact his deceased father. From the moment he walked in, I saw a huge plunger and clogged pipes in front of him. I didn't want to relay this message because I just met this man and anyway, I couldn't figure out what the heck it could mean. I finally gave in, however, and asked John if this message was significant to him. He laughed hard and then cried. He told me that he had been at his sister's house the previous week, and after using her bathroom, he had clogged up her pipes. John then went on to tell me that when he was younger, this used to happen all the time, and his father had to install brand new pipes in the bathroom to deal with this problem. The messages about the plunger and clogged pipes were just what my client needed to hear to know that his father was really there. He had a good laugh and was able to go home knowing that his father was still around him.

As shown time and time again, our departed friends and relatives don't want us to grieve for them. They are at peace and want us to feel peaceful as well. Many times they use the quickest way they know how to stop us from crying; they make us laugh. And from what I have witnessed, sometimes laughter *is* the best medicine.

CHAPTER *8*

When a Child Crosses Over

The death of a child is the death of the future.
—Emily Dickinson

Losing a child is one of the worst things that could ever happen to a person; a parent's grief is like no other. My sessions with parents who have lost a child have affected me the most, and when I first began receiving these messages, I would actually become very ill afterwards. I have since learned to "cut the cords" after I leave a reading so that this does not happen any more.

As I was writing this chapter, a number of parents who had lost their children started to call me. (As a matter of fact, I just came back from doing a reading where two friends who both lost their babies in childbirth came together for a session.) At first I thought it was a coincidence that these grieving parents were calling at this time, but now I know otherwise. However, I'm still wondering, "Am I attracting them energetically to me, are the angels or their loved ones telling them to call me because of what I'm writing about, or am I writing about this because I have been feeling that these parents would be calling me?" To be honest, I'm not quite sure what is happening. The bottom line is that it doesn't matter. The children and their parents want to connect with each other, and I'm glad I'm here to help them do it.

In this chapter, I'm going to include a few readings when young children came through to help their parents understand they were indeed okay. In the first story, a wonderful little boy named Mikey came through with messages for his parents when they were ready to hear them.

Mikey

Mikey, a little boy from my town, was lying on the ground by an athletic field when logs that were piled on top of one another rolled down and fell on top of him, ending his precious life way too soon. He was only five years old at the time, and even though I did not know Mikey, I couldn't get this accident out of my mind.

A short period of time after this tragedy, I saw Mikey's mom, Sue, in a local pharmacy. I didn't even know her at the time, but as I was passing her in the aisle, I felt Mikey around me, begging me to tell his mom that he was okay. He felt just like a little boy would, and was so excited that I was able to feel him. Because I did not know his mom, I was reluctant to do so, but I eventually knew I had to and introduced myself to her. I told her that I felt her son around me and he was telling me that he needed her to know that he was okay. She told me that she didn't even want to go to the pharmacy that day because it had been such a reminder of her beloved son since she had always gone there with him. However, after speaking briefly with her, she was relieved to have heard from her son and said that she was going to call me when she was ready to hear more from him.

It actually took a few years, but she eventually contacted me. Although she was the one who had called me, she said she was a little unsure about "doing this." I told her that I could go to her house if that would make her feel more comfortable, and she happily took me up on the offer. When I arrived, her husband and a friend of hers who I knew greeted me there. When Mikey's father saw that I looked like a normal person, I could see that he was relieved. I think he expected a gypsy-type woman with a crystal ball to be coming into his house. We chatted about things going on in town for a while, and then I felt Mikey. I asked them if they wanted to know when he came, and Mikey's parents immediately said yes.

The first thing I remember him showing me was a picture of Marshmallow Man from the movie *Ghostbusters*. I knew that Mikey was giving this message for his father, and asked his father if Marshmallow Man had meant anything to him.

"My other son and I were watching *Ghostbusters* last night," he said, now realizing that Mikey was indeed with him. "During the movie, I was telling my son that Mikey loved Marshmallow Man!"

Mikey also showed me some toys, including one that went back and forth with a weight on the bottom of it, and then he showed me a chicken. I asked what that meant, and Sue said Mikey used to put this toy on his little brother's tray and say, "Here's your chicken."

Mikey came through with many other messages as well, and he also brought other loved ones who had also crossed over with him. The whole experience made his loving family understand that we really do continue to exist after our body dies.

I also learned a lot from this reading. Since I was inexperienced at that time and my son was the same age as Mikey, I took on his parents' grief after I left and became physically ill afterwards. However, since then I have learned to clear and protect myself after doing readings, thus preventing a reoccurrence of these types of aftereffects. Now I just take with me the wonderful knowledge that the one who has crossed is at peace and is able to communicate this to his or her family.

Richard

A petite woman named Bernadette had lost her precious son, Richard, and had come in for a healing. When I began to work on Bernadette, I was relieved that I felt Richard's presence in the room after just a few minutes. He showed me a huge wide open mouth screaming, "Millie." When I asked Bernadette what this meant, she laughed and said that her neighbor's dog, Millie, was always barking, and Richard used to shout, "Millie, keep quiet!" Richard also gave other messages, which included showing me some of his toys, but I basically think he just wanted his mom to know that he was okay and was around her. I continued doing the healing on Bernadette which she needed very much at the time.

A few months later, Bernadette came back to see me with her boyfriend, her dad, and her dad's wife. Richard had messages for everyone. He was showing me that he had been putting his finger in his grandfather's ear to show him that he was around. When I asked his grandfather if he had felt anything funny in his ears, he laughingly said yes, he certainly did, and he was wondering what the heck it was.

When Bernadette's stepmother asked, "A little girl that we know has also died recently. We have been praying for Richard to be with her. Is he with her?" Immediately I heard, "*Sasha!*" When I relayed what I had received, Bernadette's stepmother confirmed, "That's the little girl's name! Thank God she's okay and Richard's with her."

During readings I take notes, and Richard gave us four pages of messages to let his beautiful family know that he was okay. He has since been persistent, urging me to call his mom whenever he wants to tell her something. One time it was just to chat because his mom wasn't doing well. As I was talking to her, he was singing, dancing, and playing the drums to The Backstreet Boys song, "Quit Playing Games with My Heart." When I told her what he was showing me, she told me that he loved to sing, dance, and play the drums to this song.

Another time I felt him urging me to call his mom. I had waited a few days before I could call her back because I had been quite busy. When I finally was able to call Bernadette, I asked her if she knew why Richard wanted me to talk to her. She told me that the following weekend she was going to be meeting the person who had received Richard's organs, and the whole week had been very emotional for her. Needless to say, she had been very comforted by her son's concern.

I continue to keep the lines of communication open for whenever Richard wants me to contact his family. Every once in a while he just wants to check in with them to tell them he's all right. He is a special child and still loves his family very much.

Bernadette, her dad, and his wife all came a second time to see me, and Richard was just as anxious to come through this time as well. As soon as they walked in the door, I heard, "Jake." Then I saw a thumb. I asked them what this meant, and Richard's grandfather said that a baby in the family named Jake had an extra thumb and just had an operation to remove it. Richard wanted them to know that he had been with Jake during the operation.

Richard also came through with many other funny messages. Among them were "Poppa snores loud" (according to his grandmother, this is quite true!), "belly button" (his granny was talking about getting her belly button pierced the day before!), "Flanders" (the day before, the same grandmother was talking about a dog from Flanders), and "Dyke's lumber sign" (his mother often passes a sign on the highway that says "Dyke's," and she always laughs at the name). Richard was the family comedian and made everyone laugh when he was alive, and still has the knack for making everyone laugh now. His loving family truly understands that his wonderful essence is still as strong as ever!

Arianna

Laura, a woman who said she had lost her infant daughter, called to make an appointment with me, but I wasn't sure if I would be able to receive any messages because her daughter had been so young when she died. Yet I still scheduled the appointment because I wanted to help Laura in any way I could.

Laura came to my office with her mother-in-law and her sister-in-law. Her father-in-law had recently crossed over and also came through with a number of messages. Finally a little girl entered the room who looked like she was about three years old. However, I remembered that her daughter was an infant when she died, so I didn't understand. When I told Laura I saw a little girl who was about three years old, Laura said that her daughter Arianna would have been three years old if she had not crossed over. Before this, I didn't realize that we grew older in the afterlife. (On the other hand, I have seen elderly people come through at a *younger* age than when they had died. With this in mind, I believe that our loved ones come through at the age they best wish to be remembered.)

Arianna's grandfather was the one who was bringing his granddaughter through. When I first saw Arianna, she was wearing a little red dress and black patent leather shoes, and she showed me a butterfly. When I asked Laura what this had meant, she told me that Arianna's brother had seen a butterfly and said that he had "just known" that it was Arianna. (Arianna was confirming that indeed it was!) Then the little girl said that her brother had been using her blanket, and she cuddled up next to him when he did this. Arianna also showed me her caterpillar and elephant toys that she seemed to like very much.

She then flashed me pictures of a police uniform and a bull's-eye. When I ask Laura what this meant, she told me that her husband was a policeman and had been taking target practice the previous day.

Arianna went on to show me a leaky pipe and her dad cleaning water off the floor. When I asked Laura what this meant, she laughed and said there was a major leak in the pipe from the sink the day before, and her husband had a hard time cleaning it up. Arianna was confirming that she was right there by her dad's side while he was cleaning up the mess!

Laura came to see me again, this time with her husband, Mark, a few months later. Right away, when Arianna's dad walked in the door, I felt Arianna's grandfather in the room. Her grandfather's name was Frank and was giving a number of messages to his son. In one message, he said the name Nico, and then he showed me a hat that felt to me as if it served as some kind of protection device for Nico. When I asked Laura and Mark if that meant anything to them, they said that a heavy freestanding basketball net fell on top of their son, Nico, and he wasn't even hurt. They believed that the hat he had on somehow protected his head. From the other side, Frank confirmed that it did, and said he was there protecting Nico when the accident occurred. After a few messages from Frank, Arianna came through and was showing me the month of April. When I asked Laura and Mark what April meant, they said that Arianna's birthday was in April. Then she showed me an Easter basket, and when I asked her parents what that meant, they told me that Easter was going to be the anniversary of her death. Arianna also showed me a pillow, and her parents confirmed that their boys had been fighting over a pillow the night before.

There were also a number of other messages from other departed family and friends, but Arianna's parents were especially thankful when their beautiful daughter had come through for them again.

These readings were a wonderful learning experience for me, as well as for Arianna's family. Even babies are fully attuned to the light and are anxious to tell family and friends that all is well on the other side. Knowing this brings so much comfort to everyone involved!

CHAPTER 9

Messages with Animals

The more you stop to observe animals and learn from them, the more healthy and peaceful you will be.

—Wayne Dyer

Many of the messages I receive are from or about animals. Because they are so unusual, many of these types of messages confirm the rest of the reading. As mentioned in a previous chapter, there was the message of the boxing kangaroo that depicted a deceased loved one who had boxed kangaroos in Australia. Then there was the giraffe with the long stretchy neck which demonstrated that a man who had such a small neck in life was now able to stretch it out as long as he desired. I already also spoke about the man who showed me a donkey to acknowledge that he indeed was with his sister when she watched a video of him pretending to be a donkey, giving rides to the children.

Receiving messages from or about animals are the easiest messages I receive. These are the messages that almost always come through very loud and clear. The next message from Griffin the llama confirmed to my client that even animals have an afterlife and want us to know that they are okay after they cross over.

Griffin the Llama

One day Donna came in to see me because she said she had a broken heart. I was going to do a healing on her, but as the healing was progressing, a huge llama that had apparently crossed over appeared before me. I didn't know whether or not to relay this message because it seemed so strange. However, I finally gave in and laughingly asked her, "You may think this is unusual, but I see a llama by your side. Does this mean anything to you?"

"That's my sister-in-law's llama, Griffin, who just died. She's going to be so happy that he's okay!" she exclaimed.

Amazing as it seems, the llama is the one who brought in Donna's brother-in-law and other relatives from the other side as well. He was a truly special animal, and he brightened up Donna's day as well as mine!

Yertle the Turtle

As I was talking to Ken, a hypnotherapist who practices at the center where I work, I clairaudiently heard "Yertle the Turtle." I asked him what that meant to him and he said that it was a song by the Red Hot Chili Peppers that he happened to have on a CD in his car. I wanted to see exactly what the message could mean, and I asked him to bring the CD inside so that I could hear it. When I listened to it, the only words I could understand on the song were, "I'm a ruler of all that I see, but I don't see enough and that's the trouble with me."

I had just been telling him to recognize the power that he had within him and to know that he could accomplish and manifest anything he wanted to. I believe his guides were reinforcing this idea by giving him the same message in a way that he could relate to and remember for a long time. After all, who could ever forget a turtle whose name was Yertle?

The Fat, Waddling Seal

Many times, the animals that are shown to me are a symbol for something else. This happened when I was in California taking a course, and a woman started talking to me about her husband. As she was speaking, I saw a picture above her of a seal who was very low to the ground, waddling back and forth. I was curious and asked her why I was seeing a seal as she was discussing her husband.

She giggled, "My husband looked like a seal. He was short, fat, bald, and had webbed feet."

Needless to say, we both had a good laugh at that one!

The Crow

A couple of times, birds appeared inside my house to give me a message. The first one occurred many years ago, when I saw an enormous crow flying around my basement. I called my husband at work to tell him about it because I felt very frightened for some reason. When my husband came home, I asked him to help me find the crow so we could set it free. When he looked around that night, the crow was gone. There were no windows down in the basement that would have enabled the crow to fly out, and there was nowhere for the crow to hide. My husband thought that I had been seeing things. However, I knew what I had seen and couldn't get rid of the fear that I had felt from it. It took me a while, but I finally understood that the crow was from the spirit world and had come to my house for some unknown reason.

About a month later, I learned from a neighbor that the previous owner of my house had committed suicide around the time that I had seen the crow flying around my basement. I know this man never wanted to move out of that house, and wouldn't have moved, if his wife hadn't forced him to. I just hope that is not the reason why he took his own life. I probably will never know the answer to that question. I do believe, however, for some reason, he took the form of a huge crow to say good-bye to the old house that he had loved so much.

The Little Bird

It's truly amazing how the angels arrange things so that I could write about them! After I had been thinking about ideas for this chapter, I took a break and went to the kitchen to get something to eat. Out of the corner of my eye, I saw something moving around in the adjoining room. As I investigated further to see what it was, I saw a beautiful little bird flying around the room. I quickly called my son and daughter who were home at the time to see this beautiful little creature. To my surprise, when my children came into the room, the bird flew to the floor and remained there without trying to fly away. As I was pulling my barking dog away, both my son and daughter began petting the bird. Now everyone knows that wild birds do not remain still if there are people near them, let alone allow strangers to touch them with a barking dog nearby. However, the beautiful bird seemed to have had full trust in them.

Although we loved the bird and wanted to keep him, we all knew that he should go back outside because that was its true home. However, the bird just wouldn't leave. We opened up the doors, and put my dogs in a different room so they wouldn't disturb the bird. Then we left the bird alone and went about our normal routine.

Eventually it flew into the laundry room; I closed the door so it couldn't escape into the other rooms, and I opened the window so that it would be able to fly outside. I kept checking the laundry room to see if the bird flew outside, but it remained in there the whole day.

Finally, later that night, I asked my son to come into the laundry room to help me make the bird go outside. Even after many attempts to encourage him to go, the bird just would not leave. Finally, as I was giving up, I remembered to ask St. Francis, the patron saint of animals, to assist the bird on its journey outside. With my son as my witness, immediately after I had spoken the words to St. Francis, the bird flew right to the windowsill, looked back at us as if to say good-bye, and then flew outside. It was a truly remarkable experience. He was now free!

Chelsea

It was a very sad day. My sixteen-year-old dog, Chelsea, was curled up in her doggie bed dying. She couldn't even lift her head as I held her and tried to comfort her that morning. I cleaned out a sticky discharge from her eyes that was preventing her from seeing. I told her it was okay to leave her body now because she was in a lot of pain, and added that she could still remain with us afterwards. I then told her I loved her, and placed her back in her bed so that she could rest.

It was snowing hard outside, and about an hour later, my son, Timmy, came home early from school. After we had lunch, he and I both went into the bedroom to see how Chelsea was doing. I started petting her, gently cupped her face with my hands, looked into her eyes and repeated what I had told her earlier, "I love you. I love you."

Immediately after I said that, Tim sat down on the bed. (I had a koala stuffed animal, along with some of my other things, in a box next to the bed because the guest room was being painted, and I had put everything from that room into boxes. My daughter, Jessica, gave me this stuffed animal to cheer me up a few months earlier because I was very sad when my son, Chris, went off the college.) As soon as Timmy sat down, the koala, which was not even on the top of the box, went off by itself and said, "I love you. I love you."

Wide eyed, Tim looked at me and said, "Mom, it's as if Chelsea said I love you back. And she said it two times, just like you did!"

Tears came to my eyes. I really believe that is exactly what had happened. Somehow Chelsea was able to relay the message back to me that she loved me too. I don't know if it was actually her, her higher self, or her angel, but it doesn't even matter. She was able to say she loved me back, and then leave her frail body peacefully two days later.

PART 2

How to Connect with the Other Side

CHAPTER 10

How to Communicate with Angels and Deceased Loved Ones

When you affirm your own rightness in the universe, then you cooperate with others easily and automatically as part of your own nature.

—Jane Roberts, *The Nature of Personal Reality*

The most important concept you must understand before you will be able to connect with angels and deceased loved ones is that we are all one. This truth, however, is too difficult to understand with the rational mind alone. At first, it may be only through meditation that you will truly be able to grasp this idea. Meditation allows you to get rid of your ego and connect with everyone else. It is when you are in the stillness of meditation that you will probably first be able to feel deceased loved ones, angels, ascended masters, and even God. After practicing meditation for a period of time, you will then be able to understand and feel the presence of these beings in your normal waking life as well.

As I teach these methods in my seminars, many are able to connect and receive messages. This is a *natural* occurrence. All of us are able to tap into this oneness and connect with it. Yes, it is a truly wonderful experience when you finally are able to receive messages and feel your loved ones and the angels. And if you can do it, and someone you know cannot, this is a good opportunity to use your expertise to show them how to do it—if and only if—they wish to know, and give them any messages you are getting for them—if and only if—they are ready to hear them. It is important not to force any of this information on others. When a person is ready, he or she will come to *you* and ask you questions.

How to Meditate

It is during meditation that you will be able to plug into your source and recharge yourself. Within six months of daily mediation, you will definitely see and feel a difference in your life. According to Edgar Cayce, when you meditate, you accumulate God energy, and you are then able to give away this energy to others. (Edgar Cayce, known as the "sleeping prophet," was one of America's greatest psychics of all time.)

Before you begin to meditate, however, I must stress the point that you should be in a peaceful state of mind. If you are not, it would be better to just say a prayer, maybe sit outside, or go for a walk. The reason is that if you are not at peace, you will probably not be able to meditate correctly, and if you do, you will be connecting to those energies that are of similar vibrations to what you are experiencing. Therefore, if you are not feeling at peace, see if the prayer or walk makes you feel better, and if this happens, you can then begin your meditation. If not, a prayer or walk in nature is equally as effective.

Set aside a regular time and place every day to practice your meditation. According to Edgar Cayce, you must first set an *ideal.* Make your ideal the highest choice you can relate to at the time, for example—peace, love, or Christ Consciousness. When you quiet your physical body through turning the mind toward the highest ideal, you will attune yourself to the Infinite.

Now you are ready. Go into a quiet room, turn off the phone, and close the door. Make yourself comfortable because you're going to be sitting or lying down for about twenty minutes. Take off your shoes and anything else that is binding on your body, including belts and jewelry. In meditation, your senses are enhanced, so you may want to burn some incense or sweet smelling candles, and put on nice, soothing music. Do whatever it is that helps you to unwind.

Guided Meditation and Techniques

Begin to relax every part of your body, beginning with your toes. Feel yourself going inside the tips of your toes. Tense and then relax them. Now do the same with your feet. Tense them and then relax. Now move up to your ankles and lower legs. Tense and relax them. Move upwards now to your upper legs and thighs. Tense them and relax. Move to your buttocks and lower back, tensing and then relaxing them. Now center your awareness on your stomach, and tense and relax these muscles. Move to your upper chest and upper back muscles. Tense them and relax. Next do your fingers, then your hands, and tense and relax these muscles. Move to your lower arms and then your upper arms, and tense and relax them. Bring your shoulders up as high as they will go, and then bring them down slowly.

Now it's time to do head and neck exercises. Edgar Cayce suggested doing this exercise because it aids the body in opening up the passageway through the throat chakra to help the energy raised in meditation to reach the upper chakras. (See more on chakras later in this chapter.)

Drop your chin slowly all the way down to your chest, and then raise it back up to normal position. Do this three times. Now drop your head as far back as you can, and raise it back up to normal position. Do this three times. Next, drop your head to your right shoulder and raise it up again. Repeat this three times. Do the same thing, but this time, lower your head to your left shoulder and raise it up to normal position. Do this three times. Now drop your head down to your chest again, and slowly circle it all the way around clockwise. Repeat this three times. Again, drop your head to your chest and then circle three times, this time moving it counterclockwise.

Now move to your face and head at this point, tensing all facial muscles, and then relaxing them. Now tense and relax the top and back of your head.

Now you're going to breathe deeply into your abdominal area, not into your upper chest. I like to also use the Edgar Cayce method of breathing before my meditations. Although it may seem complicated at first, once you master this technique, it is really quite simple. According to Cayce, this breathing exercise opens up the energy passageway to permit the intake of oxygen to stimulate the third eye and crown chakras.

With your left index finger holding your left nostril closed, breathe deeply with your right nostril. Hold this for three seconds, and then exhale through your mouth. Do this three times. Now, with your right index finger, hold your right nostril closed and inhale through your left nostril. Hold this for three seconds. Now quickly switch and use your left index finger to hold your left nostril closed, and exhale fully through your right nostril. Do this three times.

When you are finished with this breathing exercise, inhale deeply through both nostrils, hold it for three seconds, and then exhale completely through your mouth. Repeat this three times.

If You Are Not Completely Relaxed

If you are not feeling your best, a great method to use is the "vacuuming yourself out" method. Angel author, Doreen Virtue received this method when she was meditating. Ask Archangel

Michael to help "vacuum" yourself out, starting with the top of your head. Imagine you are going into the top of your head, vacuuming out any negativity or anything you don't want or need. Continue going down in your body, vacuuming out anything that is unwanted. If you feel any knot or tightness, picture yourself turning up the volume higher, and vacuum it until you feel all negativity disappear. Continue to vacuum inside your whole body. When you are finished, fill your entire body with a thick white toothpaste-like light to replace the negativity you have just removed. Fill your entire body with this light, and when you are finished, picture yourself plugging up the top of your head with a cork, so that the white light remains inside. You should feel very peaceful and lighter after this exercise.

Cutting Cords

If you still don't feel at peace, you may be feeling etheric "cords" that are connecting you to other people you have encountered. This is not a good thing because you may be feeling their energy and don't even realize it is not your own. Therefore you may wish to cut these cords.

All you have to do is close your eyes and see if you *feel* any cords attached to you. If you do sense them, mentally use a sword or whatever is necessary to sever the ties between you and the other person to whom the cord is attached. Keep cutting them until you feel they are completely severed, and ask Archangel Michael to help you. After these cords have been cut, you and the other person will feel so much better.

Sometimes while attempting to cut your cords, you may find a sword cannot sever the connection, no matter how hard you try. At that point, you may want to mentally use huge scissors or even a chainsaw to cut them! When you finally feel that you have cut the cords completely, mentally pull out their roots and replace the holes that are left behind with white light.

The Silence

Ah, finally! Now you will partake in the most important part of the meditation—the silence! The goal is to refrain from any thoughts for twenty minutes, which may seem very difficult at first. It is usually when we are quiet that we begin to think of distracting thoughts such as the errands we have to run during the day, what we are going to cook for dinner, and so forth. This is normal. Please don't get discouraged. Just allow these thoughts to enter your mind and then let them go. Trying to force these thoughts away is like saying, "Don't look at that huge elephant crossing the path." Of course you will look at the elephant! So just be patient, acknowledge the thoughts, and then let them go.

A mantra usually helps when you are beginning to meditate. Think of a phrase that you can say when you find your mind starts to wander. I have used mantras such as, "Grant me a pure heart, oh God," or "May peace prevail on earth," or just plain "Peace" or "Love." You should use a phrase that makes you feel comfortable.

Begin by repeating your mantra over and over at first. Remember though, the goal is to simply remain in silence, so after repeating your mantra, quiet your mind and experience the peace within yourself. At this time, see if you still have any knots in any part of your body. Feel yourself go within each knot and stay there, experiencing it completely. Now try to dissolve each knot with white light. Stay with it until it is gone. Do this throughout your entire body. During this whole process, breathe deeply and completely.

Let us hope at this point that you are finally feeling peaceful. Now just breathe deeply and completely, and, if need be, keep repeating your mantra. If your mind continues to wander, a very good way to silence it is to inhale deeply and hold it for three seconds and then exhale completely and hold it for three seconds. Keep focusing on breathing in this way until you just want to breathe normally and sense the silence within. You may only be able to experience complete silence for ten minutes at first. That is perfectly fine. You can eventually add a few minutes to your meditation each day. The idea is for you to experience the silence for as long as you feel comfortable. Twenty minutes is ideal.

During your quiet time you may receive messages from your higher self, deceased loved ones, angels, and ascended masters. Do not focus on these messages during the silent period of your meditation. Of course you will be tempted to do this. However, it will be *after* your quiet time, while remaining relaxed, that you may ask yourself, a loved one, or angel to answer a question you may have. A question with a yes or no answer is the best kind of question to ask. At that time, see what that small voice within you has to say. Most of the time, any information, guidance, or experience you may need will come *outside* of the meditation process as a *result* of our daily meditation. In other words, you will receive an answer later.

If You Can't Quiet the Mind

For those of you who can't seem to quiet your mind, I recommend using a guided meditation tape to take you through the process at first. A good one that I have used when I first began meditating is called *"Creative Visualization"* by Shakti Gawain. There will come a time, however, that you will just want to experience the quiet time with soothing music playing in the background.

Other Ways to Meditate

If the above ways of meditating do not work for you, I have listed alternate methods below. Experiment to find the one that works best for you.

1. Simply stare at a candle until you cannot focus on it any longer. Close your eyes, and after a few seconds, you should actually see the flame in your mind's eye. After this image disappears, repeat this exercise by staring again at the candle for as long as you can. Close your eyes and see it again in your mind's eye. Try this exercise for at least ten minutes.

2. Sit silently and feel that you are infinite. Imagine you have no boundaries. Feel the entire universe within yourself. Do this before you go to sleep, and also in the morning when you first wake up.

3. You may also try the opposite. Feel as if you have disappeared for a few minutes, and see how different it feels from being boundless.

4. Sit outside, preferably next to a tree. Close your eyes and allow the breeze to blow *through* you.

5. Practice chakra breathing. Clear out each of your chakras (see section that follows on chakras). This method is very powerful.

6. You can also tune your chakras. To do this, simply chant the following sounds: ah, a, e, i, o, u, mmm. Repeat this chant over and over for ten minutes.

7. Try a Zen meditation. Sit in a lotus position, and breathe through your diaphragm. Breathe in with the numbers 1, 3, 5, 7, and 9, and breathe out with 2, 4, 6, 8, 10. To prevent any distractions, you may want to face the wall.

8. Do whatever it is that allows you to fully relax and empty thoughts from your mind.

Effects You May Experience During Meditation

In *Meditation: The Light from Within*, author Harry Glover says that, according to Edgar Cayce, there are certain effects you may experience when meditating. They are as follows:

1. Your head may be drawn back.
2. You may experience coolness in your forehead or cool air blowing down on you.
3. You may lose awareness of your hands and feet.
4. You may feel your body swaying (externally or internally).
5. You may feel an extension of your body.
6. Your palms may get sweaty or very warm.
7. You may experience excessive heat.
8. You may experience either a lightness or a fullness in the head.
9. You may feel energy moving up or down the spine.
10. You may lose consciousness.
11. You may experience tingling in your body.
12. You may see pulsating lights.
13. You may feel pressure in your eyes.
14. You may experience time distortion. (For example, if you have only meditated for a few minutes, it may have seemed much longer. On the other hand, if you have meditated for a very long time, it may have seemed much shorter.)

You may also receive no effects, and that is perfectly fine too.

Benefits of Meditation

In the same book, Glover also mentions what Edgar Cayce said were the minor benefits you may experience from daily meditation. They are:

1. You will have an expanded consciousness and sensitivity, enabling you to become more intuitive.
2. Your memory will become sharper, and your problem solving will be improved.
3. You will sleep and relax better.

4. You will have a greater balance in your life.
5. You will have more energy and strength.
6. You will be able to tolerate yourself and others more.
7. You will have an inner knowingness.
8. You will have a more conscious awareness of the silence.
9. You will have a new attitude toward life, with more empathy towards others.
10. You will have an increased positive self-image.
11. You consciousness will expand.

You will also be able to perceive and communicate with angels and deceased loved ones.

Glover goes on to say that, according to Edgar Cayce, the major benefits you will experience from daily meditation are:

1. You will have enhanced prayer activity which will increase your personal contact with God.
2. Your willpower will be strengthened.
3. You will be able to manifest more patience, compassion, kindness, virtue, and understanding.
4. You will have more positive attitude towards life.
5. You will become a more powerful and useful channel.

Guided Meditation Tapes

As stated earlier, when I started meditating, I used guided meditation tapes. One of the tapes I used was Shirley MacLaine's *Going Within*. On the tape, she takes the listener through guided meditations and clears out the chakras. Years ago when I listened to the tape, I didn't really understand what our chakras were, but just went along with the meditations. I felt that it really helped me to relax, so I listened to the tape daily. I found that after listening to her tape for a week or so, my psychic abilities definitely increased. That is when I found out for myself that we do indeed have these energy centers within our bodies, and when we clear them out, not only will we feel better, but our natural psychic abilities become enhanced. I remembered reading about this many times, but only when I actually cleared out my own chakras did I realize this was really true.

So, What Are the Chakras?

Chakras are circles of spinning energy that we have within our bodies. In the Sanskrit language, chakra means "wheel," and although there are hundreds of them in our bodies, there are eight major ones. If our chakras are dirty or clogged, our psychic abilities are actually dimmed and may even be turned off. Thus, simply by clearing them, we can revive our natural psychic abilities.

When I describe these chakras, just imagine the various colored swirling energies inside the corresponding parts of your body, with cone-like energies extending out the front and back of your body in the corresponding areas.

The 8 Major Chakras

The first chakra, the root chakra, is ruby red in color, and is located at the base of your spine. It is the energy center that deals with fulfilling your physical needs for survival. If you have concerns about money or material needs, this chakra may be muddy and may need to be cleared.

The second chakra, the sacral chakra, is orange in color, and is located a few inches below your belly button. This chakra corresponds to your physical and sexual desires, as well as addictions.

The third chakra is called the solar plexus chakra, and is yellow in color. It is located above your belly button, and it corresponds to issues of power and control.

The fourth chakra is the heart chakra, and is emerald green in color. This chakra corresponds to all matters of the heart, including love.

The fifth chakra, the thymus chakra, is located between the heart chakra and the throat chakra, is pink in color. (Most authors don't acknowledge this one, but I have found it to be the most *important* one to clear out when trying to communicate with the angels and deceased loved ones.)

The sixth chakra, located in your throat is the throat chakra. It is blue in color, and corresponds to communication and speaking one's truth. If you have problems in these areas, you may need to work on this chakra.

Your seventh chakra is your psychic center, and is called the third eye. It is located between your eyes, and is indigo in color. This chakra needs to be perfectly cleared in order to receive messages from the angels and departed loved ones.

Your eighth chakra is the crown chakra, and is violet in color. It is located inside the top of your head. This is the center that allows you to receive Divine understanding and guidance.

Clearing out the Chakras

If you have time during your daily meditation, it is a good idea to clear out your chakras. I usually do this by imagining that I am sliding an etheric "rag" of light through each chakra; this light extends from the front to the back of each chakra. I mentally see myself stretching the rag, circling it, and clearing each chakra out. Finally I see each one as a crystal sphere of the corresponding color. For example, I start with the root chakra, and pull the etheric "rag" through it, visualizing the red cone extending out the front and another red cone extending out the back of the lower part of my spine. I then visualize the center of it as a crystal red sphere at the bottom of my spine, and see it spinning clockwise. I continue doing this with the corresponding colors to the rest of my chakras, until they are all cleared out.

A Fast Way to Clear Your Chakras

A very fast way to clear out your chakras is simply to stand up and spin. This method is included in a book by Peter Kelder which is entitled *Ancient Secrets of the Fountain of Youth*. According-ing to Peter, all you need to do to clear out your chakras is extend your arms straight out to the sides and find a focal point on the wall in front of you. Keep your eyes focused on that point as long as you can as you spin around. (This is similar to what dancers do when they "spot.") You should only spin three times at first so that you don't get dizzy, and repeat this once a day for three days. After three days, add three more spins, for a total of six spins each day for three more days. Continue adding three more spins every three days until you get to twenty-one spins. Although spinning clears out your chakras very quickly, it's important to go slowly. Since it may cause dizziness, this exercise is not for everyone.

Changing Your Diet May Increase Your Ability to Receive Messages

When I started receiving messages and actually felt the oneness of every living thing, which included animals, I just couldn't eat meat anymore. After the change in my diet, my psychic abilities increased even further. I cannot say that this will happen for everyone or that all should have a vegetarian diet. I remember that I was not at all happy when vegetarians tried to force their eating habits on me when I ate meat many years ago. All I can say is that you have to make the decision yourself, and if you do decide to become a vegetarian, most likely you will open up your third eye even further.

Chocolate, sugar, caffeine, and alcohol also seem to diminish our extrasensory perception. Try to abstain from one product at a time, and see if it enhances your sixth sense. In this way you will be able to understand how each one has been affecting your psychic abilities.

Stones and Crystals

You may want to carry a certain crystal or stone to amplify your connection to the other side. I like to carry a stone called a prehnite with me when I am doing a reading. This stone helps open up the third eye to enhance communication with angels and deceased loved ones. I also use a crystal called a phenikite which is the most powerful crystal on earth available. It is said to open the third eye and crown chakras, and it aids in clairvoyance, spiritual communication, meditation, and astral travel.

An amethyst is also an excellent stone to use because it stimulates the crown chakra, opening up communication with the heavens. I also recommend anyone doing healing work to carry a piece of moldavite, which is a green translucent meteoric glass. This is a stone of communication, and it works well with the third eye, throat, and crown chakras.

Experiment with different stones and crystals to see which ones feel right for you. What works well for one person may not be the same for another. I recommend that you go to a store that sells a variety of crystals, such as a New Age store. Select the ones you are drawn to and feel them to see if they resonate with you.

Receiving Messages

The best way to test your abilities is to try to receive messages for people you do not know. This will insure that you are being objective, since you have no previous knowledge of that person.

See if you can find someone who is willing to experiment with you. Sit across from this person, and join hands if you wish. Be still for a few minutes and try to empty all thoughts from your mind. Then just wait and see if you receive any mental pictures. You probably will receive most of your messages inside your mind's eye. At first you may think that they are only your own thoughts. Since you are just beginning, tell the person what you are receiving anyway. You may be quite surprised to learn that much of what you have believed to be your thoughts are not yours at all. Because we are all one, you may instead be picking up the other person's energies, thoughts, or messages from their loved ones and angels.

Ways to Receive Messages

You may receive messages in a number of ways. If you are a visual person, you will probably receive the messages in pictures, or *clairvoyantly*. Or else you may hear certain messages, which means you will be experiencing them *clairaudiently*. On the other hand, if you feel certain things, for example, if you feel heat or coldness or sense something around you, you will be experiencing these messages *clairsentiently*. Or you may just have a gut feeling or an inner knowingness. In this case, you will be experiencing these messages *claircognizantly*.

Whichever way you receive them, just acknowledge everything you get, even if it doesn't make any sense to you. What doesn't make sense to you may be extremely significant to the other person. Especially remember to accept even the most bizarre messages because these may be the most significant of all!

Symbols

You may receive some messages in symbols. At first they may seem difficult to interpret, but try to figure out what the symbol means to you. For example, if you see your Aunt Anna in your mind's eye, it could be a person named Anna coming through or even the other person's aunt. Don't give up—it usually means something. The departed loved one may be using *your* frame of reference to give you messages.

One time when I was giving a reading for a woman, in my mind's eye I saw the old television program *Bonanza.* I asked the woman if Bonanza meant anything to her, and she said no, she was too young to have ever seen that show. So I quickly went within myself and tried to figure out what Bonanza had meant to me. All I remembered from that show was some man on it with a name that sounded like Hass. I relayed the name "Hass" to her, and she said that a man named Hass had put her boyfriend in jail. If I hadn't further analyzed the seemingly unrelated "Bonanza," I would have missed an important message.

Remember to accept whatever you are given and don't question it. If you get a message with specific names such as Hass, or see strange pictures like a boxing kangaroo, the person will go home knowing without a doubt you have received a message for them.

Also, when you first receive messages, you may think you are simply reading someone's mind. I thought that may have been happening to me at first, but then I realized that some of my clients didn't know what some of the things I received had meant until they went home and asked someone else. Other times I received messages about events that happened when the clients were very young, so they certainly hadn't been thinking about such things for a very long time. I have also received messages from those the clients didn't even know had died until after they left my office and had made some phone calls to see if these loved ones had indeed crossed over.

Calling on Angels, Ascended Masters, and Deceased Loved Ones

You may want to experiment with calling on different ascended masters and angels. Before I do a reading, I call on four Archangels to help me. I ask for them one by one so that I can sense what each one feels like. First I ask Michael to come, then Uriel, then Gabriel, and then Raphael. Each of these angels feels a little different than the others. Sometimes one comes in stronger than another on a given day. (Uriel has been coming through a lot for me lately because Uriel is the peace angel and is promoting peace at this most critical time.)

If you want to, you may then call on departed loved ones too. They will feel very different from the archangels, but in this way you will be able to experience how each one feels, so that when you do receive a message from a loved one who won't give you a name, you will still be able to know who he or she is.

When you do this exercise, you will see that the ascended masters and angels really do come when you ask them to! Many people feel guilty calling upon these wonderful beings because they think they are taking them away from someone else who needs them more than they do. This is not true at all. Because they are spirits, ascended masters and angels can be in more than one place at one time. All you need to do is ask them to come and they will be there for you!

Loved ones, on the other hand, will come if they are able to come at the time. Sometimes they are actually performing tasks on the other side, such as helping others cross over, so they may not come at the exact time you ask them to come. Do not be discouraged. It is the same as when they were here on earth and were busy and could not come to visit you when you wanted them to. Just be patient and they *will* come to you when they can, sometimes when you least expect it.

How They May Come to You

The easiest way to receive messages from your loved ones and angels is in the dream-state. The only problem is that if you don't wake up after a dream, you will not remember it. So before you go to sleep and you ask your loved ones or angels to enter your dreams, be sure to ask them to wake you up afterwards. Be persistent, and even if you don't dream of them right away, continue to ask them to come to you on several consecutive nights. Remember, they *will* come when they can.

Also look for signs around you, such as the bumper stickers or license plates of cars that cut you off, billboards, songs on the radio with messages that seem to be just for you, objects flying off shelves, and so forth. Our loved ones who have crossed over may give messages in unexpected ways, so just be aware of what is going on around you at all times. A loved one who is finally able to communicate with you will be so happy to have finally made that connection too, and you most likely will experience a *wonderful* peaceful feeling when that connection is made!

Most people who come to see me have felt their deceased loved ones in some way and just need confirmation that it was really them. Others tell me that a friend or relative had received messages from their loved ones and wonder why they aren't coming directly to them. I always tell them that if their loved ones are coming through to others, they probably have been trying to come directly to them as well!

Sometimes we dismiss signs and messages either because we are not paying attention or we think the messages are just our thoughts. The first messages I received came through simply as thoughts. This is the way our loved ones communicate with us—telepathically, and we often cannot separate our thoughts from theirs. If a random thought comes into your consciousness, it could very well be someone trying to communicate with you. Trace your thoughts and see if you can figure out how the thought originated. If you cannot pinpoint it, it may very well be a message from a loved one trying to talk to you. At this point, try to quiet yourself and listen. You may receive more thoughts, words, pictures, smells, or even feelings. Ask the person who it is and listen. This is where the benefit of meditation comes in. If you have been meditating, you will be able to quiet yourself easily and fully experience what is being given to you.

Okay, you are now able to communicate with angels and deceased loved ones! Remember that practice makes perfect, so the more you practice the techniques I have mentioned, the better you will get at receiving messages. Be patient with yourself and don't force anything to happen. Just allow it to happen and it will.

Meditation to Connect with Angels and Deceased Loved Ones

Below is a guided meditation to help you connect with angels and deceased loved ones. You may want to tape this meditation using your own voice for maximum effectiveness.

Close your eyes and get into a comfortable position, either lying down or sitting up with your spine straight and your feet flat on the floor. Take a nice long, deep breath, hold it, and then let it go like a sigh of relief. Do this one more time. Inhale slowly, hold it, and then let it go like a sigh of relief. Good!

Now we're going to do the head and neck exercises Edgar Cayce recommended. First, drop your chin slowly all the way down to your chest, and then raise it back up to normal position. Do this three times. (pause) Now drop your head as far back as you can, and raise it back up to normal position. Do this three times. (pause) Very good! Next, drop your head to your right shoulder and raise it up again. Repeat this three times. (pause) Now do the same thing, but this time, lower your head to your left shoulder and raise it up to normal position. Do this three times. (pause) Excellent! Now drop your head down to your chest again, and slowly circle it all the way around clockwise. Repeat this three times. (pause) Finally, drop your head to your chest and then circle three times, this time moving it counterclockwise. (pause) Wonderful!

Next we're going to do Edgar Cayce's breathing exercises. With your left index finger holding your left nostril closed, breathe deeply with your right nostril. Hold your breath for three seconds, and then exhale through your mouth. Do this three times. (pause) Now, with your right index finger, hold your right nostril closed and inhale through your left nostril. Hold your breath for three seconds and with your left index finger, hold your left nostril closed and exhale fully through your right nostril. Do this three times. (pause)

When you are finished with this breathing exercise, inhale deeply through both nostrils, hold it for three seconds, and then exhale completely through your mouth. Repeat this three times. (pause) Excellent!

Now just feel yourself drifting, floating, relaxing more and more. (pause) Feel your awareness going now into your root chakra which is located right at the base of your spine. See it as a beautiful ruby red sphere of light. Focus on this beautiful red color for a moment. (pause) Now surround it with God's white light. (pause) Good!

Now focus on your sacral chakra which is located a few inches below your belly button. Go within yourself and see it as a beautiful orange color. Focus on this bright, clear, orange color for a moment. (pause) Now surround it with the beautiful white light of God. (pause)

Now bring your awareness on your solar plexus chakra which is located a few inches above your belly button. See it as a lovely yellow sun shining brightly within you. Remain focused on this yellow color for a moment. (pause) Surround it with pure white light. (pause)

At this time, move up to your heart chakra. Feel it and see it as a beautiful emerald green color. Remain focused on this chakra for a moment. (pause) Now surround it with the white light. (pause) Good!

Now move on up to your thymus chakra, which is located right between your heart and throat chakras. See it as a beautiful pink color, and focus on this color for a moment. (pause) Now surround it with a white sphere of God's light. (pause)

Next, move up to your throat chakra. See it as a beautiful sky blue color and focus on this color for a moment. (pause) Now surround this chakra with pure white light. (pause)

Okay, now move up to your third eye chakra, which is located right between your eyes. See it as a beautiful indigo color and focus on this color for a minute. (pause) Surround it with God's light. (pause)

Finally, move on up to your crown chakra which is located at the top of your head. See it as a beautiful violet color and focus on this color for a moment. See this violet light extending all the way up into the heavens. (pause) Now surround this violet color with the white light of God. (pause) Very good!

At this time you are ready to call upon the Archangels one by one to guide and protect you. Feel and experience each one as they enter the room.

Say, "Archangel Michael, please be with me now." Remain focused on any feelings you may be experiencing at this time. (Take as much time that is needed to experience his presence.)

Now say, "Archangel Raphael, please come join me in my meditation now. Thank you so much." Focus now on Archangel Raphael's energy. This is the way he will feel to you whenever he is in your presence. (Pause to feel his presence.)

Now say, "Archangel Uriel, please come by me now. I am honored by your presence." Focus now on the energy of Archangel Uriel. Remain in this peace for a moment. (Take as much time that is needed to feel his presence.)

Finally, call upon Archangel Gabriel and say, "Archangel Gabriel, please enter into the room right now. Help me to feel your presence." Focus on his presence for a moment. (Take as much time that is needed to fully experience his presence.)

At this time you may call on any ascended masters, saints, or other archangels, and feel their presence one by one. (Take as much time that is needed.)

You are now ready to connect with your loved ones who have crossed over to the other side. Ask your loved one who you wish to contact to come into the room right now. Be patient and wait to feel his or her presence. (Take as much time that is needed.) Talk to your loved one and tell him or her anything you wish to say. Take your time. (pause) If you have a question, ask it now. Become aware of any impressions, thoughts, pictures, smells, colors, or feelings you receive now or even later on in the day. (pause)

Ask your loved one to come to you in your dreams and to wake you up afterwards so that you will remember them. Thank your loved one for coming today and know he or she will always be there for you.

Tell your loved one whatever else you want to say at this time. (pause) At this point, you may say good-bye, knowing you will be able to connect with him or her whenever you want to from now on. (pause)

And when you are ready, take a nice deep breath, and let it out like a sigh of relief. Focus on your body and the room you are in. (pause) At your own pace, slowly open your eyes, feeling peaceful and refreshed, remembering everything you have just experienced.

CHAPTER 11

Teenagers Receive Messages after a Group Meditation

*When we raise ourselves through meditation to what unites us
with the spirit, we quicken something within us that is eternal
and unlimited by birth and death. Once we have experienced
this eternal part in us, we can no longer doubt its existence.
Meditation is thus the way to knowing and beholding the
eternal, indestructible, essential center of our being.*

—Rudolf Steiner

As I stated in the previous chapter, meditation is the key to
opening up your psychic abilities. Quieting yourself and listening
enables you to experience the oneness of everyone and everything. When you are able to experience this oneness, not only
will you will be able to connect and receive messages from those
still here on earth, but you will also be able to receive messages
from those who have crossed over, the angels, and ascended
masters as well.

Although I personally knew the power of meditation, I was
looking for some tangible evidence to prove what I was saying
was true that I could tell my clients and friends. The search
didn't take long! I was able to obtain this evidence very quickly
from a Sunday meditation class I had taught at the request of my
daughter, Jessica, and her friends. The class consisted of nine
teenagers—six girls and three boys.

I taught them the Edgar Cayce method of meditation and
explained to them that the quiet time was the most important

part of all. After going through all the preparation for the meditation, I asked them to experience complete silence for ten minutes. I told them to repeat a mantra which we agreed upon before the meditation if their minds wandered at any time during the meditation.

After the ten minutes of silence was over, they were all completely relaxed and felt wonderful. At this point, just for the heck of it, I wanted to see if they would be able to receive messages. To my surprise, *each and every one of them* was able to receive messages after the silence!

They were also able to see auras after they opened their eyes. I stood up and asked if they could see mine. I told them not to focus above my head, but to look beyond it. Within a few minutes, *everyone* in the class was able to see it. While some saw it only as white, others actually saw colors. They also were able to see that my aura moved at a slightly slower rate than the movement of my physical body.

While they were still pleasantly relaxed, I broke them up into groups of two, with one group of three. I told them to hold hands with their partners and quiet themselves another minute to see if any messages came to them. I explained that at first they may not be able to distinguish between their thoughts and the messages they were receiving, but to tell the other person whatever impressions they received anyway. I never expected every person in the room would be able to do this right away, and yet they all did! And this was the first time most of them had ever meditated.

One of the girls in the group, Dana, received a few messages for her partner, Alyssa. At first, Dana said she kept getting the name "Roger Rabbit" in her head and asked Alyssa if that meant anything to her. Alyssa was surprised and said that she and her friend were just talking about the Roger Rabbit movie the day before. Then Dana said the name "Smith" popped into her head, and Alyssa immediately replied that Smith was her best friend's last name. At that point, Alyssa was able to receive a message for Dana and she said that the name "Chris" popped into *her* head. Dana was amazed and immediately told Alyssa that Chris was the name of a very good family friend.

Then my daughter, Jessica, received a message that at first she believed to be insignificant. She said, "I'm getting a very strange name," she paused and then said, "Tecumsah." Stephanie, another girl in the class, gasped and told Jessica that Tecumsah definitely meant something to her. Stephanie said she had to do a lab on genetics in biology class, where each student pretended to have a husband and a baby. She had named her baby Tecumsah and her other friend had named her baby Hasmucet, which is Tecumsah spelled backwards.

A week after the meditation class, the Tecumsah saga continued. Everyone in Stephanie's history class was told to do a research paper on a specific Indian, and the teacher asked Stephanie to write about the Indian Chief Tecumsah!

Then ... a week after being assigned the Tecumsah project, Stephanie came over to my house to visit Jessica. She was telling me about all the Tecumsah incidences and about her project. I was amazed at all these so called "coincidences" and for some reason I then remembered that my son Chris loved the Indians when he was much younger, and had a collection of Indian books in the basement. I went down to find them, but since it had been many years since anyone had looked at those books, I couldn't locate them at first. Finally, as I was looking in the bookshelves, I glanced down. There on the floor by my left foot was a book entitled *Tecumsah the War Chief*. I screamed for Stephanie to come down quickly to look at the book that was on the floor. We started laughing hysterically and I fell to the floor. Then when we were finally able to calm down, we tried to figure out what the whole thing had meant.

I believe that Tecumsah is one of her guides and is trying to get her attention. At first we didn't understand why a war chief would want to contact Stephanie, since she is a pacifist. Stephanie came to the conclusion that since Tecumsah has crossed over, he has since learned that war is not the way to go, and to atone for his warlike deeds, he is now trying to encourage Stephanie to promote peace on earth.

Stephanie also received messages during the meditation group for Joao, a boy who was sitting next to her in the class. Stephanie almost didn't say it because she thought it was insignificant, but I told her to tell him anyway. In her mind's eye, she said she saw a bag of Skittles candy and asked Joao if that meant anything to him. He said that it certainly did because he loved Skittles and bought them every day. Apparently, they were very expensive in Brazil where he's originally from, but he now takes advantage of their price and buys them here all the time.

As I was listening to Stephanie tell Joao about the Skittles, I started receiving messages for Joao. I felt a baby named Mary was with him. I asked him if that meant anything to him and he said yes. When he was younger, he had a baby sister named Mary who had died.

Mary gave Joao a few messages, including that he shouldn't feel guilty about her death and that she was in a very good place. Apparently, Joao's mother had thought Mary couldn't go to heaven because she hadn't been baptized before she died. Mary was telling him that this wasn't the case at all; she was in heaven right now and was at peace. She loved her family so much and just wanted her family to be at peace also. Mary also showed me a blanket (which I found out weeks later was very significant to Joao's mother because she had carried this blanket around with her a long time after Mary had died).

Joao was so happy that his sister had come through and now told me about a message he had received earlier. After the meditation, he said he had heard the name of a song that his dad used to sing to him and his sister when they were little. Now we understood that his sister was probably the one who was reminding him of this song, trying to tell him that she was there.

After speaking to Joao, I then went back and asked Stephanie, who was sitting next to him, to continue to talk about her other psychic experiences. She went on to tell me that after the meditation, when I told them all to ask themselves a question that could be answered with a yes or no answer, she felt her whole body tingle and then turn numb. She said her cheek muscles felt as though they were being lifted, which forced her to smile, and then she saw a glowing yellow light.

Another student from the class, Steve, was also excited because he was able to see everyone's aura so clearly and was able to do things he never thought he'd ever be able to do. He emailed me and said that he had a good time in the class and asked if I could give another one soon. I told him I'd be very happy to oblige!

The meditation class was a success and even turned out to be an afternoon of messages. Jessica and her friends learned the importance of meditation in receiving messages and realized that continued meditation would enable these messages to come in even stronger and more frequently for them.

And so it would be for you too! Not only is daily meditation the key to obtaining peace within yourself, but it is also the key to opening up your third eye to receive messages. The results from the Sunday meditation class were a *perfect* example of this.

PART 3

Is There More
to Life Than This?

CHAPTER 12

The Soul Survives

Since the soul represents parts of the human being that are not physical, it cannot get sick, it cannot die, it cannot disappear. In short, the soul is immortal.

—Rabbi Harold Hushner

As shown by loved ones who have crossed over, the "other side" actually is the real world, and when our body dies, we return to this real world from which we came. Therefore, life does not begin at birth and end at death. This is just what the mass consciousness has wrongly believed for thousands of years. All our fears about death are based on a lie—that we are our body. The fact is that we have a body, but we are not a body. We are not human beings having spiritual experiences, but rather, we are spiritual beings having human experiences. Our essence which is our soul, survives and just our shell, our body, dies.

So, what happens to our soul when our body dies? Does it go to heaven or hell, or even purgatory? What actually happens is that we create our own heaven or hell, not only here on earth, but also after we cross over. We judge ourselves at the end of each lifetime and determine how we have progressed, or if we have accomplished our life's goals. God does not judge us. God is a loving God, and since He created us, he knows that we are human and are going to make mistakes. We therefore determine our own fate.

Yes, we do "atone for our sins," but we will judge ourselves after we face the reality of our actions. We will be the ones who will want to make amends for what we have done, for we will want to return to a state of perfection which is our birthright. We all have God's essence within us, and whenever we have done something that is not of a loving nature, we just lose sight of this reality. That is all. Only in the state of pure love do we remember who we really are.

After we have crossed over, we focus again on our souls and not on our bodies, and are able to see things the way they really are. God is not waiting at the Pearly Gates for us when we die to throw us into the fire. God is love, and He would not do that to us.

The Master Jesus said that heaven is not "out there," but instead, the kingdom of God is within. So, if God is within all of us, in reality, we are all one with God. Our separateness occurs only in our minds. When we aren't loving to others, because we are all one, not only does it hurt *them*, but it hurts *us* as well.

When someone who has crossed over comes back to give a message to a loved one, most of the time he or she is very much at peace and wants loved ones to know that. The rare times that souls are not at peace are when they are remorseful and want to be forgiven for something they have done or if they need to resolve some issues. Sometimes they will choose not to move on until their loved ones forgive them and these issues are resolved.

Also, when spirits come through, they feel exactly as they did when they were alive. If they were funny, they are still funny; if they were loud, they are still loud, and it is easy to receive messages from them; if they were quiet, they are still quiet, and it is very difficult to hear them; if they were not so nice, their energy feels the same, and their presence feels very uncomfortable; if they had a loving presence, they still feel wonderful. I could go on and on, but the reality is that we don't automatically become saints when we cross over. We take what we have learned when we were here on earth, and carry it with us to the other side. And since we evaluate our lives, we may choose to come back again, to do it better. Remember, we want to return to our true essence, which is pure love, and if that means coming back here to learn the things we didn't learn the last time around, we may want to try again and again until we "get it right."

The most important thing we need to remember is that we are all connected to each other. We will therefore feel the energy we put out to others because we are all one. And this goes for the good as well as the bad that we put out into the world. Our actions affect others in more ways than we realize, so we should try to make a positive difference in the lives of everyone we meet. Not only will we feel better now, but we will also be at peace after we have crossed over to the other side.

The Souls of Animals

I couldn't write this chapter without talking about what happens to the souls of our beloved pets after they leave their bodies. Just as human souls survive, so do the souls of the animal kingdom. These wonderful creatures actually stay around their owners for a long time after their crossing. And according to those who have had "near-death experiences," pets often were among the first to greet them after they left their bodies.

I have had many experiences of receiving messages from animals; many times the animals actually give me their names and even show me their favorite activities and toys. At first I was surprised at what I was receiving because, after all, animals do not normally "speak" to us in the same way humans do. However, these experiences showed me that pets are much more aware than we realize of what goes on in their lives and are anxious and able to communicate with their owners after they have left their bodies. They want their owners to know they are still with them and love them very much.

When my dog Chelsea died, the vet gave me a pamphlet to read which talked about how we can deal with our grief after losing a pet. I found it very helpful, until I read something I certainly did not agree with. It said that there were a number of normal things that owners experience after losing their pets. One sentence stated, "One of the most disturbing yet normal signs of grief is an hallucination of your pet. 'Hallucination' means you think you hear, see, feel, or smell your pet's presence in brief flashes." I shook my head in disbelief as I read it. The reason that it is "normal" to experience seeing, feeling, or smelling our pets is because they actually *do* come to us.

I laugh at the ignorance of the scientific community. Just because they cannot *see* a human or animal spirit, they do not believe it is there. Yet many of the things that cannot be seen, such as God, angels, air, love, and peace are the most important things of all. I genuinely *want* them to do more research on life after death so they can see for themselves that the soul never dies.

As I was writing the previous paragraph, in front of me I saw a vision of a flattened earth. I immediately knew what the angels were telling me. Hundreds of years ago, people thought the world was flat and laughed at those who had thought otherwise, but how wrong they were! It is the same with anyone who does not believe in the existence of God, the angels, and the eternal soul.

I do know one thing for sure—after they leave their bodies at the end of their lives, the skeptics will see for themselves that they had been wrong in denying the existence of their eternal soul. If they would have understood this beforehand, it would have brought them and their loved ones so much more comfort and peace when they were still here on earth. Oh well, it's better late than never!

CHAPTER *13*

A Loving, Universal God Who Doesn't Abandon Us

God is more truly imagined than expressed and He exists more truly than He is imagined.

—Saint Augustine

God is the focal point in my life. The more I pray and meditate and the closer I get to God, the more I receive messages and Divine Guidance. Those of some strict religious persuasions say that becoming psychic and receiving messages are against God's will. Without a doubt, I know within myself that it is quite the opposite of what they say. Of course, it is everyone's right to believe what he or she wants to believe. Just as I tell everyone, always look within yourself too, and see what feels right to you. If someone, including myself or even a religious leader, tells you something, always question if what he or she is saying sits right with you. If it does not, do not listen to what they are saying. Let your conscience be your guide. Do not believe something just because someone tells you it is right or wrong; listen to your own guidance, to God within you. This knowingness will always bring you a sense of peace. This peace is God's way of telling you that He is there, and He is guiding you.

God speaks to all of us, not just the leaders of a church. I learned this long ago when I just couldn't understand why the heads of various churches each said their church was the only right one; some even went on to say that those of other faiths would burn in hell after they die. This whole concept just felt awful to me. No way could this be true, I thought. God is a loving God, and He loves everyone—after all, He is the creator of each and every one of us.

Those of you of the Christian faith know that even Jesus questioned some of the rules and regulations of his faith. This didn't sit well with the religious leaders of that time. He was also able to perceive the future, perform healings, and often saw and spoke of angels. And more importantly, he often said, "This and more can you do if only you believe." He never said he was the only one who could perform miracles; he said we *all* could if we had enough faith.

Since I read the Bible over and over when I was younger, I often questioned why the church would pick and choose what they shared with the congregation. When they would turn the loving words of Jesus into fire and brimstone, I wanted to get up and scream, "No, it's not that way at all!"

God is not waving His finger at us saying how bad we are. When we do something that we feel is wrong, we just know within ourselves that it is not right. The reason for this guilty feeling is not because God is judging us, but because we are judging ourselves. When we step away from what we truly are, which is all-loving, we step away from God, and it feels just awful. The reason it feels bad is because, when we do something physically or emotionally harmful to ourselves or others, we have momentarily disconnected from the love that we are, and we also disconnect from the part of ourselves that is connected to others. Of course, we don't know this consciously, but we instead feel it subconsciously.

On the other hand, if we do something considered good, for example, when we help others without expecting anything in return, we experience a peace within ourselves. This is because the goodness resonates with the God that is within us. This feeling is what we are most familiar with, the love that we are.

When we share or feel love, we experience God and we subconsciously remember who we really are. When we help others, we also feel good because, since we are all one, in reality, we are helping ourselves as well.

When Something Goes Wrong in Our Life and We Blame God

In my work, I often deal with those who have experienced tragedies in their lives. Many times, they become angry with God because of these tragedies and wonder how God could have allowed them to happen. On the other hand, these same people often feel guilty that they are mad at God. In reality, however, the bottom line is that God did not cause these so called tragedies to occur, nor did He ignore their prayer requests.

Everything that happens in our lives is a learning experience for the growth of our souls. Sure, we could learn life's lessons in easier ways, but sometimes we do not listen until there is a crisis. During various times in our lives, our souls may create events such as illnesses which force us to wake up and make changes we wouldn't otherwise have made. Sometimes illness enables us to get the rest we desperately need, make the move we really want, quit the job we hate, get the divorce from our unhappy marriage, or do whatever else we need to do. If we would have listened to that inner knowingness beforehand, chances are the event or illness would not have occurred.

What I strongly recommend is for us to be still and ask God to help us understand everything in a better way. When so called "bad" things happen, sometimes our first reaction is to blame God and ask, "Why me?" However, throughout all our sorrow and helplessness, God still shines through for us and never abandons us. Often when bad things happen, something good comes out of it in the long run. I've heard this time and time again.

It is in our most difficult hours that we need to feel God's love the most. We need to tell Him that we want to feel His presence stronger. We can ask as many angels as we feel are necessary to help us get rid of anything that is preventing us from feeling God's peace. Remember God and His angels *want* us to feel this peace again.

We can ask God to let us know what we need to do in order to get well or to make the situation better. We then need to quiet ourselves and just listen. We *will* receive an answer. The key is that we need to be willing to do whatever is being shown to us and act upon it. Yes, God is there, and He always was, but He will not force us to do anything. We have to make the decision to take whatever action is necessary for our own peace as well as for the peace of others.

God does answer our prayers, but not always in the way that we want them answered. If we pray for someone else to get better, for example, and it is not in the Divine plan for that to happen, we may get angry at God if the person does not get well. However, since we are not able to see the whole picture, it is difficult to understand what the other soul needs to go through at the time; only God and the higher self of the other person know the answer to that. And even though God may not have answered the prayer in the exact way we wanted Him to, God will help carry the person for whom we are praying through the seemingly difficult times and create inner peace in his or her life.

"Footprints in the Sand" by Mary Stevenson (11/8/22–1/6/99)[1] says it the best. I'm sure most of you are aware of this inspirational poem:

---

[1] Mary Stevenson grew up poor and lost her mother when she was seven during the Great Depression. In 1936, when she was locked out of her home, she observed a cat leaving footprints in the snow. She begged God for his guidance during one of her down times and eventually wrote "Footprints in the Sand" when she was fourteen. Mary gave handwritten copies of her inspirational poem to others, but didn't secure a copyright for it until she was encouraged to by her friend, Kathy Bee, in 1984.

FOOTPRINTS IN THE SAND

One night I dreamed I was walking
Along the beach with the Lord.
Many scenes from my life flashed across the sky.
In each scene I noticed footprints in the sand.
Sometimes there were two sets of footprints.
Other times there were one set of footprints.
This bothered me because I noticed that
During the low periods of my life when I was
Suffering from anguish, sorrow, or defeat,
I could see only one set of footprints,
So I said to the Lord, "You promised me,
Lord, that if I followed You,
You would walk with me always.
But I noticed that during the most trying periods
Of my life, there have only been
One set of prints in the sand.
Why, when I have needed You most,
You have not been there for me?"
The Lord replied,
The times when you have seen only one set of footprints
Is when I carried you."

Yes, there is light at the end of the tunnel, and that light is
God's light. We shouldn't give up on Him because he never gave
up on us. We need to remember that he never has and never will
abandon us, and when we need Him the most, He will carry us
through it all. All we need to do is ask Him to grant us peace and
strength in any situation. We may not always understand why
things happen now, but after we leave our bodies, we will finally
understand the whole picture.

CHAPTER *14*

Angels

He will give his angels charge of you to guard you in all your ways. On their hands they will bear you up, lest you dash your foot against a stone.

—Psalms 91: 10-11

When an angel comes through with a message, it feels quite different than a message from a loved one who has crossed over. An angel's essence is much stronger, and does not have a "human" feeling to it. As messengers of God, angels have a higher vibration than those who lived here on earth in a body. Their energies radiate pure love and peace, while our loved ones who have crossed over feel just like they did when they were here on earth.

Guardian Angels

All of us have at least one guardian angel, and some of us have more than that. Guardian angels guide and protect us throughout various stages of our lives (although different angels join us as we go through various changes in our lives). Because we have free will, the angels cannot intervene in our lives without our permission. If we want some help with anything, we just need to ask the angels for their assistance and they will be there for us. It really is that simple!

Protection from the Angels in a Car Crash

When my older son, Chris, first obtained his driver's permit, I asked the angels to surround his car and protect him whenever he drove. On the first Christmas after getting his permit, he volunteered to drive my family to my in-laws' house, which was about forty minutes away. As we were getting ready to climb into my car, I noticed that it had a flat tire. Because of this, we were forced to use my husband's car instead, which was bigger and sturdier than mine.

Just a few blocks from our house, as we were stopped at a traffic light on the main road, a drunken driver plunged into us from behind at full force. We were all fine, but as I climbed out of the car to inspect the damage, I was surprised to see the other driver's car was totaled and our car had only a very tiny scratch on the bumper.

If we had used my smaller car, things certainly could have been much worse. But then again, I remembered the angels were with us, and I believe we would have been totally protected anyway.

Angel Intervention in the Selection of a College

My daughter, Jessica was a senior in high school and was in the process of applying to different colleges where she could major in dance. She came into my room to announce that for some reason she did not feel good about applying to one college which was located in New York, even though it had one of the best dance programs in the country, and she didn't understand why. As Jessica was telling me this, I saw the figure of a huge angel standing about a foot away from her. Excited, I told my daughter what I was seeing, and went on to tell her that she was probably having this feeling about the college because she felt the angel telling her not to apply there. I told her to listen to what she was feeling and not apply to that college, even though logically it did not make any sense. She ended up applying "early decision" to a college in Connecticut and was thrilled when she received an acceptance letter from that school. She was not supposed to go to the college in New York at all. The angels had Connecticut in mind for her instead.

Angel Stops Runaway Shopping Cart

A few years ago when my youngest son Timmy and I were getting out of my car which was parked by a supermarket, we spotted a shopping cart rolling down hill, ready to make its way onto a busy street. Without a doubt, this could have caused an accident, so I quickly prayed out loud, "God and the angels please stop that cart, now!" Immediately the cart just stopped, right on an incline! There had been no one near the cart when this had happened. When I turned to see Timmy's reaction, and glanced back at the cart, a man came out of nowhere and moved the cart onto a speed bump. Again, I turned to see Tim's reaction, and when I quickly glanced back at the cart, the man was gone!

Excited, I exclaimed, "Wow! Tim, that was awesome!"

He just looked at me, and because he was so used to me talking about angels and miracles, he said, "Yes, Mom, it was an angel," as if it was an everyday occurrence. And he was right—it was!

Angels Help Me with My Angel Seminar

I could go on and on with other angel experiences since I allow angels to be such a significant part of my life. However, I will share just one more at this time. A few years ago, I was preparing my notes one day for the first angel seminar I was going to be giving. I was just about finished, but I still needed a good conclusion for the program. At that point, I definitely needed a change of pace and was very tired, so I decided to take a break and go to the local K Mart and then the Grand Union.

After I had finished shopping, I packed all the bags in my car and headed home. The shopping center was about fifteen minutes from my house. When I had been halfway home, I felt an angelic presence in my car telling me that I left my purse at the supermarket. Not believing this at first, with my right hand, I began rummaging through all the bags as I was driving to see if my purse had been in the car after all. One would think at this point I would have listened to the message right away, but I didn't. Finally, when I realized that the message I received was genuine and I really did not have my purse with me, I quickly turned around to go back to the shopping center.

Panic set in and I began repeating, "God and the angels, please allow my purse to be protected." When I finally arrived at the Grand Union, I ran inside and asked the cashier, and then the person behind the service counter if they had found a purse. They both said that they did not. Then all of a sudden I felt an incredible peace come over me.

It was very busy outside the store because it had been lunchtime and there were cars and people everywhere. I was guided by an unseen force which took me to the center of the parking lot. To my relief, I spotted my purse on the seat of a shopping cart! People had been passing it by, not even noticing it, as if the cart and my purse were invisible to them! I quickly grabbed my purse and got into my car, crying like a baby.

The peace that I felt at the time was incredible. I knew without a doubt that the angels had made sure that my purse was totally protected. They were really there for me. And on top of that, I now had a wonderful angel story that I could use at the end of my angel seminar. The angels truly are amazing!

All We Need to Do Is Ask

As stated before, the angels are ready to assist us, but most of the time, they must wait for us to call upon them. Often they come to us simply as a thought, a feeling, a knowingness, or a vision. At first we may feel that we are only imagining the messages we are receiving. Therefore, all we need to do is ask God to allow us to know when the angels are truly giving us messages. These prayers will not go unanswered because God wants us to be able to feel and hear His heavenly messengers.

Unfortunately, many times we unknowingly cut off communication with the angels because we fear what we might see, feel, or hear. Because of this, the angels will not come to us because they want to bring us comfort, not fear, so they will wait until we are ready for them. In this case, we may want to pray for God to help us release any fears that are preventing us from connecting with our angels.

At other times, we may feel unworthy and therefore do not call upon them for their help. I assure you that we are all worthy of their assistance. It doesn't matter who we are or what we've done; the angels are there for us. They are not here to judge us, but simply to guide and protect us at all times.

We may also call on as many angels as we feel are needed in different situations and they will all come. Also remember that they can be in more that one place at one time, so we are not taking them away from another who needs them more than we do.

Archangels

The archangels have a more powerful, stronger essence than guardian angels. They oversee and guide the other angels who are with us on this earth. The exact number of archangels is debatable, but the four that are the most widely known are

Michael, Gabriel, Raphael, and Uriel, and these are the ones I call upon the most.

Michael

Archangel Michael is the patron saint of police officers and soldiers. His main role is to take away negativity in various situations. We may call upon Michael whenever we feel negativity within or around us, and simply ask him to cleanse away this negative energy. Michael is able to restore harmony and peace, and will come to help us whenever we call upon him. He is a very huge, powerful angel, and is often seen by those who are clairvoyant as an indigo (purplish-blue) colored light.

Gabriel

Sometimes Gabriel is depicted as a male and sometimes as a female archangel. For simplicity, however, I will just use the masculine pronoun when describing him here. Gabriel is the angel to call upon if we need help writing or speaking because he is the communication angel. All we need to do is ask him to help us overcome any fears or problems we are experiencing in communication, and he'll be there to help us. Clairvoyants often see him as a copper colored light.

Raphael

Raphael is the angel we would call upon to heal ourselves or others, except in cases where an illness is part of the overall plan. When we ask for a healing, Raphael may not only show us what we can to do get well, but he often may show us how our thoughts and actions had triggered our health problems in the first place.

Raphael also guides and protects travelers. We can ask him to bestow upon us a safe and healthy journey, and he will indeed be there. Some clairvoyants see him as an emerald-green colored light.

Uriel

Uriel aids us in situations when we feel helpless and comes to the rescue during disasters. Archangel Uriel helps us to fulfill our life's purpose, and pushes us to feel motivated when we are in a slump.

Uriel is ever so present to help out during times of war and violence. Whenever I meditate or pray for peace on earth, I feel his strong presence. Clairvoyants see him as a whitish-yellow colored light.

I call the four archangels my buddies because I talk to them all the time. They recently assisted me during a very rough period in my life, and certainly came through for me. (This story is included in the next chapter on healing.)

We can call upon the archangels and the other angels as well at any time and they *will* come. Remember that they can be in more than one place at one time, and no job is too big or too small for them. They are very real beings of God's light who are here to shine for all of us. They bring us protection, comfort, relief, and understanding far beyond what mere words can express here. I am so grateful to God for sending us these wonderful heavenly messengers.

CHAPTER 15

Healing

*So neither ought you to attempt to cure the body without the soul;
and this is the reason why the cure of many diseases is unknown
to the physicians of Hellas, because they are ignorant of the whole
which ought to be studied also; For the part can never be well
unless the whole is well.... For this is the great error of our day in
the treatment of the human body, that physicians separate the
soul from the body.*

—Plato

"Truly, I say to you, he who believes in me, the works that I
do, he will do also; and greater works than these shall he do;
because I am going to the Father." (John 14:12). Since my
childhood, I have always held onto these words and instinctively
always knew that I would one day be able to perform some of
these works which included healings. (As a matter of fact, *every
one of us* is able to do these things as well, because we *all* have
God within us.)

When my children were younger and if they were hurt or
sick, I instinctively practiced "hands-on healing" on them. I felt
the angels around me when I was performing these healings,
telling me where I should place my hands. This also happened
when I worked on my pets.

My Dog, Chelsea

A few years ago when I came home from a meeting at my
children's school, my daughter, Jessica, informed me that some-

119

thing was wrong with my dog, Chelsea. The dog repeatedly collapsed when she tried to stand up, and it looked as if she had broken her front leg. I sat with her all night, holding my hand on her leg, saying, "Thank you, God, for healing Chelsea," knowing that she would be healed. Still, the human part of me was ready to bring her to the vet in the morning to fix her wounded leg.

The next morning, when I woke up, however, I glanced down from my bed and saw Chelsea standing up. She was looking up at me, as she did every morning, telling me she wanted to eat. As I walked into the kitchen, she ran alongside of me, just as she always did. Her leg was healed, and she was as good as new.

This showed me that one does not have to believe the healing is going to work for one to be healed. My dog did not know what I was doing to her the previous night. Her paw was healed even though she probably thought she was just relaxing with me as I was watching television.

Confirmation of Being Healed by the Angels

As I was writing this book, I was going through quite an ordeal of my own and needed a healing myself. Although I help people every day with different types of problems of the body, mind, and spirit, I was taken off guard when I received the news of two different lab results from my yearly gynecological exam. Within a few hours of each other, I received phone calls from two different doctors. Not only did my pap smear come back with abnormalities, but my mammogram showed calcifications which were not present the year before. I needed biopsies for both areas, and to be honest, I was quite worried. Of course I should have had more faith, but when I was in the middle of this inner turmoil, I couldn't get rid of the negative thoughts that kept going through my head.

I went for the biopsy of the uterus, and to my relief, the results came back normal. However, I had a few "problems" with my breast biopsy. The doctor went in to remove the abnormalities with a fine needle biopsy three times, but on each try, the calcifications moved away from the syringe. The doctor said that in all the seven years she had performed these biopsies, this had never happened before. Needless to say, this continuous "probing" was causing me tremendous discomfort. I took a deep breath, and finally asked the angels to help. Right after calling upon the angels, I realized that I needed to give myself permission to release this "unwanted" area inside of me. As soon as I affirmed to myself that it was okay for the area to be taken out, the doctor was finally able to remove the cells.

I wish the story ended here, but it did not. The results of this biopsy showed that the cells they removed were abnormal and more needed to be removed via surgery to make sure it wasn't cancer. I just couldn't believe this was happening to me.

A few days later, my son was home from college. He drove me to get my younger son at his school, and then we were going to a basketball game. I sat in the back of the car because I knew my younger son would want to sit in the front with his older brother. While I was in the back seat, I called on the four Archangels—Michael, Raphael, Uriel, and Gabriel—to give me a sign that everything was going to be all right.

As soon as I finished my silent prayer, my son turned around to me and said, "Hey, Ma, check out the license plate in front of us!"

I leaned over to get a better glance, and through my tears I was able to see, "4 Angels" written on the license plate. I truly believe it was the four angels confirming they had heard my prayer and everything was going to be okay. I was relieved, at least for a while.

A few days later the human part of me started questioning everything again, and I wanted another sign. I was so frightened and tried to keep it all inside because I didn't want to worry my family and friends. I know now that "stuffing everything down" made it even harder for me. During this time, I wasn't practicing what I had been preaching—that I needed to listen to messages from the angels and know they were truly there. I had already received a powerful message, so why did I need another one? All I know is that when I was going through this whole ordeal, I was totally numb and it was hard for me to open up to anything.

I started doing Reiki and energy healing on myself every day. On some days, the energy that came out of my hands was so hot and on other days, nothing. One afternoon, I was very tired and needed to take a nap. I put my hands on the area that needed to be healed and the whole bed started to shake. I thought my sheepdog, Oreo, was on the bed and was breathing heavily, causing the bed to go up and down. (She's a big dog!) However, when I glanced down, she was on the floor on the other side of the room. The energy that was coming out of my hands was so hot that my whole body was drenched from perspiration. Even though the energy was so warm, I felt very good and peaceful. I kept my hands on the area for a long time until Oreo began to bark in the kitchen, telling me she had to go outside. I didn't want to get up, but I knew I had to because Oreo would have had an accident in the house. I removed my hands from the troubled area, and the energy that was coming out of my hands immediately subsided.

Surgery was scheduled for the following week, but I felt within myself that I was okay and didn't need the surgery. After a lot of praying and meditating, I called the doctor's office and cancelled my surgery. However, the human part of me still wanted to make sure I was doing the right thing, so I scheduled another appointment with the doctor to ask her some questions. Because there was a doctor's strike, I couldn't get an appointment right away and needed to wait another month. It was a very long month for me and I started to question everything again.

It seemed like forever, but the day of the appointment finally arrived. I was anxious to find out the answer to an important question I wanted to ask the surgeon. "I know the cells are abnormal, but what are the chances that it is cancer?" She replied, "I won't know until I remove the section and perform another biopsy on the surrounding tissue." She then added, "In all the years I have practiced medicine, only two people chose not to have this surgery. One of them did not have cancer and the other one did."

Needless to say, when I heard that, I became frightened and scheduled another date for the surgery. The panic set in again. Why wasn't I listening to the angels?

A few days later, it was snowing hard outside and I was at a service station waiting to get gasoline when a car cut me off on the gas line. Instead of getting angry at the driver, I just "knew" I should look at the license plate. I quickly put on my windshield wipers because I could not see out of the window due to the heavy snowstorm. I glanced over the snowy dashboard and read the license: "NOE 44U." Noe is my last name, and since I was forty-four years old, I thought the angels were saying, Noe, you're 44. I thought, "Why would they be telling me that? I know that already!" However later that day when I told my friend what I saw, she immediately understood what it meant and interpreted it for me—Noe, 4 angels 4 you! I knew she was right. The four archangels were telling me they were there for me again. I laughed and tears began rolling down my cheeks. I felt relieved again, but then after a few days, I began to worry again. Yes I know—how many signs did I need to get before I believed the angels? I always talked and listened to the angels, so why was I not listening to them now when I needed them the most?

Finally, the day of my surgery arrived. Bobbie, a friend of mine who went through the same ordeal a year before, came with me. The old saying that "laughter is the best medicine" is certainly true! She made me laugh the whole day, so I could not even think about what was going to happen next.

A nurse came in to ask me a few questions. "Did you eat or drink any fluids today?" "Do you drink?" "Smoke?" "Do drugs?" As I answered no to each question, Bobbie interrupted and said,

"I definitely wouldn't be able to pass that test!" Both the nurse and I laughed hard.

Then the nurse took my vital signs; my temperature was 99.2 and my pulse was 99.2. Although I didn't pay attention to it, the nurse pointed out that 992 was my special number. Bobbie wanted to play that number in the lottery that day. However, I remembered Doreen Virtue's book, *Healing with the Angels*, had a section on what different sets of numbers meant. I mentally made a note to remind myself to look up those numbers when I got home.

When the nurse left, Bobbie tried to get me to drink water because I was thirsty, but I kept telling her that I was not supposed to drink before surgery. She tried to convince me that nobody would know. She also wanted me to glance in the other room because an elderly woman was taking her teeth out. She then went on to tell me a story about when her mother was having an operation and they couldn't find her teeth when she woke up. All I know is that I couldn't even think about what was going to happen to me that day because Bobbie had been distracting me all day long with her funny stories.

Finally, as the nurse was wheeling me down the hall to surgery, Bobbie ran quickly alongside of us. "Tell them to put breast implants in there, since you'll be opened up anyway."

The nurse and I laughed. "I'd love to borrow your friend for a day," the nurse said. "She is *so* funny!"

"Yes, she certainly is," I replied, breathing a sigh of relief for having Bobbie with me that day.

I told Bobbie to please go home now because I was going to be a while, but she would not hear of it. She stayed at the hospital, greeting me when I came out of the anesthesia with some more jokes. After a short period of time, I felt fine and when I was given permission, she drove me home.

When I got home, I looked up what the numbers 992 meant in the angel book. It said, *"If you've recently suffered a loss, expect it to be replaced in the very near future. Everything is working in your favor, although there may be so much behind-the scenes' activity involved that you wonder if God has forgotten about you. Worry not! Feel the energy of your life, which is moving forward right now. You are not being punished by your recent loss. The universe is, instead, preparing you for newness."* Was this still another sign by the angels telling me that everything was going to be all right?

I had to wait over a week for the results of the tests. This seemed like the longest week of my life. Finally, on the following Wednesday night at 8 PM, the surgeon called me at home.

"I have good news for you," she announced. "It's not cancer."

I was so relieved, I started to cry. "Thank you so much! I'm going to kiss you," I exclaimed.

She laughed and said, "No, please don't do that." She then told me what else I needed to do and then we hung up.

The angels had been trying to convince me all along that I was going to be all right. So why didn't I listen? In the midst of everything, even though it was difficult to see past my "problems," the angels were always there guiding and protecting me.

Whether or not I had healed myself from cancer or whether I even had it at all, I will never know. I do know that I needed to go through this so I now could tell those who come to me, "Yes, I really *do* understand what you're going through because I went through it myself. God and the angels are always there for you, in good times and in bad. Just keep the faith and *know* this is true."

Mental Patterns in Illnesses

According to Edgar Cayce, what one thinks and feels emotionally usually finds expression in the physical body. Much of what Cayce discussed in his readings was about the preventive measures people could take to stay well. For example, he often recommended the following principles to remain healthy: maintain a well-balanced diet, exercise regularly, keep positive thoughts, relax and have fun, and keep the physical body cleansed on the outside and on the inside. He affirmed that being healthy meant coordinating the physical, mental, and spiritual aspects of life.

This is so true. We need to understand that illness does not just "happen" to us. Because we are not just a body, but instead are a combination of mind, body, and spirit, we need to realize that our negative thoughts and feelings really do create imbalances in our bodies. If we maintain happy, healthy, peaceful thoughts, we will create in ourselves happy, healthy, and peaceful bodies. All we need to do is change our way of thinking if we want to create a peaceful life for ourselves and others.

Focus on Your Feelings

Quiet yourself and focus on your feelings at the present moment. Understand that what you are thinking right now is creating your present reality. Hopefully you are having peaceful thoughts at this time. If you are not, simply reprogram your thoughts to reflect the kind of life you want to lead right now. By doing this, you will be taking full responsibility in creating your own heaven here on earth and you no longer place the blame on someone else for how you are feeling.

I highly recommend Louise Hay's book, *Heal Your Body A–Z* which describes the mental causes for physical illnesses and the various ways to overcome them. When I experienced the ordeal with the breast biopsies, I immediately looked up what it meant in her book, and it was right on target. It said that the probable cause was putting everyone else first, and a refusal to nourish oneself. This was so true! Only after everything was over and I knew I'd be okay did I truly comprehend the importance of nourishing myself. After all, if I was not feeling well, I could not be of service to anyone else.

Louise Hay also says that we need to dissolve the mental causes of our illnesses. (She had firsthand experience in this when she healed herself of cancer by getting rid of her old resentments.) She explains that so called "incurable" diseases are only those that cannot be cured by *outer* methods. In these cases, the healing can occur when one decides to go *within* and makes the changes that need to be made.

Author Wayne Dyer says it perfectly, "When you are told that you have some kind of physical affliction, you can either prepare to suffer or prepare to heal." When you are willing to change your negative patterns to positive ones, you are automatically preparing to heal on every level. See yourself perfect and healed, and you *will* create that reality for yourself.

Listen to guidance from God and the angels and don't ever doubt they are there for you. Don't beg God to make you well, for that would mean that you don't believe it's possible. *Know* God is making you well *now* and thank Him for it. Feel it, know it, and have no doubts. When you have this level of faith, you will just *expect* a miracle to occur and it *will!*

CHAPTER *16*

We Are One with the Universe

A human being is part of a whole, called by us the Universe, a part limited in time and space. He experiences himself, his thoughts, and feelings as something separated from the rest— a kind of optical delusion of his consciousness.
—Albert Einstein

Many of you already have an inner knowingness about the following subject. However, there will be those who will find the following information hard to accept. I always tell my clients and students to go within themselves. If it feels right, accept it. If it does not, do not accept it. That goes for anything anyone ever tells you. *Always* go within for your answers.

The universe is vast. I find it very difficult to believe that the earth is the only planet in the entire universe with life on it. Perhaps we are the only planet with life as we know it, but certainly not life in general. It just does not make any sense for the universe to be so limited.

So let me get right to the point. Not only do I believe there is life elsewhere—I *know* there is. In addition to being in touch with "the other side of the veil," I have also been in contact with beings that have not originated from the earthplane. One such incident occurred when I was meditating and a wonderful loving presence entered the room. I opened my eyes and saw a small being that I knew was not human standing in front of me. All I

128

can remember other than it had huge eyes was the tremendous sense of peace I experienced when it stood there. I felt as if I had known this entity and it knew me; it was sending me so much love that I began to cry. It was totally unlike the "aliens" we see on television who want to take over the earth. I felt as if it knew so much more than those on earth did about peace, love, and human respect. If we of earth would only know of this peace, there could never be war again.

I was reluctant to tell anyone about this occurrence because I didn't think they would understand, and after a while I even started to question what I had experienced. However, after hearing confirmation of the existence of other lifeforms from author Doreen Virtue, I didn't disregard my knowingness any longer.

Meeting Doreen

Years ago when I began my spiritual journey and read all the books I could about spiritual enlightenment, I found some books on hypnosis and saw how effective quieting the mind and listening to affirmations was. I then decided to become a Certified Hypnotherapist so that I could help other people realize the power they had within themselves. During that time, I received a flyer in the mail from the American Institute of Hypnotherapy stating that Doreen Virtue, a gifted author of numerous angel books, was teaching courses on Spiritual Counseling in New York. I felt I was being pushed strongly by a higher source to take these courses, and enrolled in her program.

From the moment I stepped into the classroom, I realized that I was divinely guided to meet Doreen. (Before meeting her, I had been praying to be led to someone who would help me expand the intuitive gifts I had been given since my experience with the light.) She took us all through many exercises to open up our "third eye" (our psychic center), and taught us how to communicate with deceased loved ones and angels. Although I had already been receiving messages from departed loved ones and angels, I needed to fine-tune the methods I used to receive such messages, and her suggestions helped me enormously.

Towards the end of the course, Doreen talked about incarnated angels, starpeople (those from different planets or galaxies), and walk-ins who live on the earth right now. As she was speaking about this, she glanced at me as if to tell me I was one of the above. I didn't understand it at first. However, during the break, I walked up to her to ask her if she was saying that I was one of these types of beings. She explained that the angels told her that I was a walk-in starperson. My first reaction was, "No way!" That was crazy. However, she told me to go within and ask the angels myself. She told me to ask them before I went to sleep to come in my dreams to tell me who I was and where I was from. I asked the angels to come that very night, but I didn't receive any answers right away. I was persistent though, and made the same request the next day, and then the next. I also told them to wake me up after they came to me so that I would be able to remember the dream. (If we don't wake up after our dreams, we don't remember them.)

My "Dream"

Finally, after a few days, I had the most incredible experience. I dreamt that a man with a long ponytail who had his hands extended to heaven asked me to pray with him. He began to recite the Lord's Prayer and asked me to extend my hands upwards also. After repeating each line to the prayer, I felt as if I was being zapped by a huge bolt of electricity. Because of the forceful sensations I experienced, I knew this was more than a dream.

I immediately sensed he wasn't from "here" and asked him, "You're not from the earth, are you?"

He responded, "No, Lucina, I'm from where you are from," as he looked directly into my eyes with a piercing look.

"And where is that?" I inquired, knowing this was going to be the answer I needed.

"Andromeda," he answered quickly, stressing the long "o" sound in the word Andromeda.

A strong peaceful energy then made its presence known in the room with me, telling me to pay attention to what the man had just told me. With that, my dog, Chelsea, jolted me awake when she started to gag by my bedside; I was then able to remember the whole "dream."

I remained in bed for a while trying to absorb the information I had just been given. Remembering my request to the angels, I immediately thanked them for their intervention.

So what was I going to do with this information? And could this information really be true? This was way too much for me to grasp all at once. I do remember though, that it all made so much sense to me. During the last few years, I have often felt that I did not belong on earth because I just could not understand many things that go on here, especially war and violence. As a matter of fact, I am oversensitive about violence. One time, when I received a gun catalog in the mail, I immediately called the customer service line and told the woman to please take me off their mailing list. When she asked me why, I quickly responded, "Because I do not like guns!" Feeling guilty because I thought I had raised my voice, I apologized to the woman on the other end of the line. For those who know me, that was the most assertive I get. But it is in areas dealing with guns, war, and violence that I speak up the most.

When I later asked Doreen via email about those from Andromeda, she responded quickly and said they have specific characteristics. They love animals and children, but mostly, they cannot tolerate violence of any kind. She also said that they are soft-spoken and try to quietly help people one by one as they come into their lives. That certainly sounded like me. (Doreen often talks about starpeople in her books. I highly recommend any of her books, but especially *Earth Angels* which goes into the most detail on this subject.)

Others Like Myself from Different Dimensions

Now let me go one step further. Perhaps my soul *has* originated from another area in the universe. Am I the only one? In all my dealings with hypnosis and receiving messages, reincarnation comes up quite often. So if our souls do not die, and we choose to come back, why would we choose to keep coming back to earth? Surely, if we have lessons that need to be learned here, we would come back here, but if we want to experience different levels of understanding, could we choose to go to different planets and galaxies? If this is the case, I certainly cannot be the only one who has experienced life elsewhere. Maybe you have also. However, this is something that only *you* can answer.

Just as people from different cultures on earth behave differently and have distinct customs, it is the same as those from different areas in the universe. There are all types of souls— peaceful, warlike, civilized, uncivilized, and so forth.

We may think that those of the earth are so advanced, but could there be those from other planets who are even more advanced than us? I'm not talking about being more advanced in technology, but more importantly, I'm talking about being more advanced in human compassion, love, and understanding. Can people from earth really understand what love and compassion means if they continue to fight and create war?

Is it possible that we can learn from other dimensions, just as we can learn various aspects about life from different cultures on earth? I believe the answer is yes, we can! Although we may not remember who we are, I believe there are many of us on the earth right now from other dimensions who are trying to bring peace back to our beautiful planet.

As stated over and over in this book, in reality, we are all one. This includes being one with the entire universe. What we do here on earth not only affects the earth, but the entire universe as well. When we are at peace, the entire universe, on some level, experiences this peace as well. However, if we had a war and used bombs and other weapons of mass destruction, not only would we be destroying the earth, but if these weapons went out into space, we would be destroying other areas in the universe as well.

I affirm that those in higher dimensions will not allow this destruction to occur. For one thing, they have been sending us souls who remember, even if it is only on a subconscious level, that peace must prevail. Sometimes they send us these souls as babies, and at other times these souls may choose to come as adults so that they can immediately do what they came here to do. In this case, a soul may come as a "walk-in," where it makes an agreement on some level with another soul to use its body to be of service to humankind. This is *not* the same thing as a possession, where a negative entity takes control of a body without the permission of the original occupant. A walk-in is usually an evolved loving entity who has an important mission to accomplish right now. (Many times a walk-in does not even know that he is one. He just knows that he acts and feels like a totally different person than what he used to be, and he usually has higher ideals than he normally had before.)

Of course, we do not need to be a walk-in or a starperson to promote peace on earth. Those of us on earth can work together to protect our wonderful planet and the universe as well. When it comes down to it, it does not matter where we are from. What matters is that we are here now. And by being here now, each of us can make a positive difference in this world.

As spiritual beings, we are love and nothing else. Any negative emotions or feelings are just an illusion. (I encourage everyone to read *A Course in Miracles* which discusses this further.) I know this is difficult to understand, but it is the truth. Each of us, no matter where we have originated from, has God within us. This means that in reality we are all pure love and peace, and any negative emotions or activities are just distracting us from doing what we came here to do.

In Part 4 of this book, I will go into more detail on exactly what we can do to create peace both within and outside ourselves. For now, it's enough to say that because we are all one, we are one with the universe as well. We must remember that we of the earth are not the only living beings in the universe. So let us allow peace to prevail on earth, and in so doing, we will be allowing peace to prevail in the entire universe as well.

CHAPTER 17

Reincarnation

What the entity is today is the result of what it has been in days and experiences and ages and aeons past. For life is continuous; and whether it is manifested in materiality or in other realms of consciousness, it is one and the same.

—Edgar Cayce

Our souls are eternal; after our physical body dies, we may choose to go to other realms or we may choose to come back here to experience lessons we need to learn. According to Edgar Cayce, the main goal of reincarnation is to become aware of our true spiritual nature and how we are connected to everyone and everything. The process of obtaining this state of awareness may take us many, many lifetimes. However, according to Cayce, in reality, there is no time; it is only in our three-dimensional sense that time exists.

My First Past Life Regression

When I became a Certified Hypnotherapist, the instructor asked if anyone in the room wanted to get rid of a phobia. I immediately raised my hand because I had been extremely fearful of water, to the point that I could not even put my face under the water when I took a shower. At that time I believed I was afraid of the water because I almost drowned in the bathtub when I was just an infant. I truly believed this accident affected me subconsciously, making me fearful of water the rest of my life. I was about to find out that my fear had much earlier roots.

The instructor asked me to sit on a stool in front of the room. He went through a relaxation induction, and then asked me to go back to the time when I first became afraid of water. Then he asked me if I had reached that point. He had thought I would go back to that point in my current life which brought on my phobia.

He questioned, "Karen, Karen, are you there yet?"

I didn't answer. He asked again. I still gave him no response.

Finally, I whined, "Stop calling me Karen. My name is Isabelle!" The other students in the class later told me that my voice had totally changed to that of a little girl.

Shocked, the instructor went on to ask me, "Okay Isabelle, please tell me what year you are in, and why you are afraid of the water."

"The year is 1042 and I am in Norway on a wooden boat with my whole family. We are a group called the Vikings," I replied.

He told me to go to the part when my fear of water began. I began seeing each member of my family fall into the water and drown one by one as I watched. When the instructor asked me what was happening, I began sobbing. It was too traumatic for me to even talk about it. He quickly went on to tell me that I was to watch the scenes only as an observer with no feelings attached. I was then able to tell him what I was seeing.

He explained to me that I could now release my fear because this incident happened hundreds of years ago and was no longer relevant to me in this life. Eventually he was able to bring me back to the present time, and although I didn't understand it, I felt a lot better.

The next morning I was able to take a shower with my face in the water. Within a month, I was even capable of taking swimming lessons in our backyard pool with an instructor from the local YWCA. Before the regression, I had not even gone in my pool and would never consider taking swimming lessons. (I must admit though, I still do not enjoy going in the water and still have to work on this issue.)

After the hypnosis, I came to two conclusions about my regression. The first is that I actually went into a past life experience. In that case, my water phobia had been carried with me from life to life, ever since the year 1042. The other conclusion I came up with is that I had a spirit, Isabelle, who was around me my whole life, and I could not distinguish her fear of the water from my own. However, both of these explanations satisfy me and I believe both of them can be true. All I know is that my fear of the water lessened after the regression, and for that I am thankful.

We Don't Just Die

With all that I have been through in my life, of this I am certain. We do not just die. We may even choose to come back over and over again to learn the lessons we need to learn. The lives we chose to live may just be here on earth, or they may be somewhere else. Wherever we choose to go, we go in with the knowledge that we must accomplish certain things. If we leave that life without doing what we chose to do, we will somehow *know* this, for we will not feel fulfilled.

Family and friends usually choose to come back all at the same time so that they can be together again. This may explain why we may sometimes feel so drawn to others even though we have just met them. They may seem "familiar" to us because we *did* know them in a previous life.

The same thing goes for those with whom we have unresolved issues. We may have chosen to come back because we needed to resolve our issues with them. Therefore, if we don't want to deal again with certain people who were at odds with us in this life, we must get it right this time around. If we make peace with everyone now, we will be a lot happier both in this life and in our future lives as well.

How to Find out about Your Past Lives

You may feel drawn to a certain area or region before you have ever have been there, or feel like you already know a specific person you have just met. You may dislike someone for no apparent reason or feel drawn to a specific time in history. You may have specific fears, loves, and talents of which there is no known origin. All these experiences may have been the results of your previous lives. These experiences have made you what you are today, and are instrumental in creating who you will be tomorrow.

The easiest way to find out about your past lives is to be regressed by a qualified hypnotherapist. He or she will take you through relaxation exercises and then bring your awareness to a past life that was significant in explaining who you are today. All you need to do during the hypnosis is to be able to relax completely. When you are regressed, the life that was the most influential and needs to be faced at the present time will probably come up. You will be able to remember everything from the regression even after you awaken from hypnosis. You will be experiencing it as an observer only, without any of the feelings from the previous life. Many times, just reliving past life incidents will bring to the surface how certain fears and phobias began, and you will then be able to release them.

During the regression, you may think you are making up the information you are receiving. Thoughts and pictures may be brought to the surface of your mind for you to sort through, and you may not be able to distinguish these "past life thoughts" from current thoughts. This is normal. Just be willing to accept whatever information is being shown to you and you can analyze everything later.

More information may continue to surface during the next few hours and even days after the regression. Pay attention to whatever you feel is important and sort things out in your mind. Remember that you don't have to allow negative past life experiences to affect you any more. Your current life is what really matters now.

Focus on the Present Time

Although it is true that our past life experiences have influenced us greatly, let us focus instead on who we are now and who we can become. If we do it right in this life, then we won't have to make amends later. Let us help others, promote peace, be kind to all living things, and protect our beautiful planet. By doing these things, we can make a positive difference in this world *now* and not have to worry how our actions have negatively affected others at a later time.

PART 4

May Peace Prevail on Earth

CHAPTER 18

Peace on Earth

Lord, make me an instrument of your peace.
Where there is hatred ... let me sow love
Where there is injury ... pardon
Where there is doubt ... faith
Where there is despair ... hope
Where there is darkness ... light
Where there is sadness ... joy
O Divine Master,
Grant that I may not so much seek
To be consoled ... as to console
To be understood ... as to understand,
To be loved ... as to love
For it is in giving ... that we receive,
It is in pardoning ... that we are pardoned,
It is in dying ... that we are born to eternal life.

—St. Francis of Assisi

Earlier in this book I mentioned that my whole life had changed after I experienced the light—when it spoke to me and said, "Luce lucina, bella luce lucina, which means light, little light, beautiful little light." At the time, I was perplexed as to why this angel was speaking to me in Italian. I thought perhaps it was one of my deceased relatives, since my family on my father's side was Italian. However, I have since learned that this wonderful light actually was that of a very humble man who had once lived in Assisi, Italy in the thirteenth century. In his earlier years, this man was very wealthy, but decided to give up all his possessions so that he could dedicate his life to God. This gentle man could communicate with animals and responded to negativity with love. This humble spirit is one of my guides at this critical time on earth. His name is St. Francis, and he, along with other angels, including Archangel Uriel are guiding many of us at this time to promote peace on earth.

Peace Begins Within

Each of us can make a difference in this world and can actually create the peace that was intended here on earth. However, we first must experience peace within ourselves; only then can we create peace outside ourselves and affect others in a positive way. This sounds so simple, and once we put our hearts and minds to it, it really is!

Let me explain further. As I mentioned many times throughout this book, you are one with everyone and everything. You are not separate from God or from others, and even though you may be only one person, your thought forms actually do affect others in a big way. If you have negative thoughts, those around you who have similar or lower vibrations are constantly being reinforced by these thoughts. On the other hand, when you have positive thoughts, you influence everyone around you in a positive way. In other words, negative energy cannot penetrate into the higher levels of energy, but the higher levels of energy can penetrate into the lower levels. This is because positive energy has a higher and stronger vibration than negative energy, which has a slower and weaker vibration.

Because of the oneness of everything, harmful or negative ideas and activities in one part of the world really do affect those on the other side. If these thought waves are filled with love, they will make others feel good, and this vibration of love will in turn create acts of kindness. On the other hand, some waves are negative and create anger, greed, violence, and other negative energy. These thought forms are drawn to similar thought waves all over the world and merge with them, creating the ripple effect of even more negative energy.

So again, even though you appear to be separate from everyone else, you are really linked together to other thought forms at all times. Your thoughts are energy, and energy is real. If your thought forms are loving, you can actually achieve peace, not only for yourself, but also for the entire world. It makes sense then, to say that if you want peace on earth, you must first remember to keep your own thoughts on peace and harmony. And here's the clincher—because positive thought forms have a stronger and higher vibration than negative ones, if you begin to change your own negative thoughts into positive ones, this will in turn raise the vibration of the entire world!

How Do You Begin?

You must first practice releasing your negative thoughts and attitudes, which not only disrupt your own peace of mind, but also the peace and harmony of the entire world. If there are bad events taking place around you, you must understand that they actually are manifestations of your own thoughts. You need to begin anew and visualize the situation you want to create with totally new, positive thoughts.

If you meditate daily, you will sense when there are negative thought forms around you that did not even originate within yourself. You will then be able to change these thought forms to positive ones, neutralizing the energy within and around you. If you feel negative in any situation, simply pray for inner peace. Your negative thoughts will then turn into positive ones, and you will begin to feel uplifted. This inner peace will eventually extend to your family, friends, neighbors, your city, state, country, the world, and even the entire universe.

The next time someone with negative thought forms disrupts your peaceful mind, call upon the angels to help you. Ask

Archangel Michael to surround the room you are in with as many angels that are needed to get rid of the negative energy that was sent your way. Then call upon the angels to surround the person who is infringing upon your space and send him peace too. The only way to put a stop to the ripple effect of negative energy is to begin a new ripple effect of positive energy. The other person will not consciously know what you have done, but subconsciously he will. He will feel the positive energy directed his way and will cease to feel the need to direct negativity in your direction. Try it. It really works!

If, on the other hand, you respond to negativity by sending it back to the person who has directed it to you, this negative cycle will continue, and you will eventually receive this same energy back. If you send love instead, the negative cycle will end, and everyone involved will feel so much better.

All of us want peace in our lives. So if we direct a higher, more powerful energy of love in response to hate, not only are we creating peace within ourselves, but we are also extending this peace to others as well.

Just as Albert Einstein had once said, "Nothing happens until something moves," we need to do something to change our way of thinking and acting in order to become an instrument of peace. In this way we can create the peace that is very much needed on earth, or else hatred, war, and violence will continue to exist. Begin your new way of positive thinking today. Your life will be so much better from it, and so will the lives of everyone around you.

How can you change your negative thoughts to positive ones? Remember that whatever you think about expands. Therefore, you just need to watch what you think beginning right now. Think positive thoughts and use your energy to expand upon what you want, which is peace, not on what you don't want, which is war. Because we are all one, begin now by cooperating with one another. Help as many people that you can during each and every day. Instead of just worrying about how events will affect just *you*, understand how your actions will also affect others. If you extend this new energy of love and concern towards fellow human beings, you are creating peace both within yourself and on the earth as well.

The Power of Prayer

It is important to *pray* for peace too. Remember that when you pray for peace, you should feel the peace as if it is already occurring in the present moment. Create a positive statement such as, "Thank you, God, for allowing peace to prevail on earth," and know that whatever is needed to obtain this peace is happening now.

Do not beg God for peace—instead, thank God for peace. If you beg, it means that you don't believe it will really happen. Feel that your prayer for peace has been answered, and it will be so!

The Illusion of Being Separate from God and Others

As perfectly stated by author Wayne Dyer, somewhere along the line, we have created the illusion that we are separate from God and from others. We have created the illusion that we are what we have or what we do. We have created the illusion that we need to be better than others. We have also created the illusion that because we are separate from our Source, we do not have the power of the Source. This incorrect way of thinking has prevented us from experiencing the total love and peace that we truly are. We need to wake up and remember who we are right now!

In truth, we are all connected. We are still one with God and with everyone else as well. Because of this, we can create bliss in our lives and spread peace not only within ourselves, but also in the lives of those around us. Whatever we put out into the universe, we receive it right back. Because we are all one, when we extend the peace within us to those around us, we will experience it coming back to us a thousandfold.

A statement from *A Course in Miracles* says it best: "If you have a problem, it is only the belief that you are separate from your Source." When we remember that we are one with God, we are able to realize that we can actually create everything in our lives. Although we are not as powerful as the entire Source, we are indeed a part of it and retain the power that the Source has. Since this is so, we are able to perform miracles in our lives as well as in the lives of others, and that includes creating peace on earth.

We are Unique within the Oneness

Although we are all one, we each carry certain truths and experiences within us. Even though one hand has five fingers on it, none of the fingers are exactly alike, and they each have a different job to do for the hand. So it is with each of us. Although we are all connected to God, each of us has a different reason to be here on earth. None of us is exactly like another person. Therefore we must accomplish what we chose to do when we came here, not what another person wants us to do. We need to go within ourselves and seek our own truth.

In order to experience peace within ourselves, we should always question everything that comes into our awareness from outside ourselves and see if it feels right to us. Even though we may say we believe certain ideas, if the information doesn't come from within ourselves, we may experience an element of doubt about these views. What is true for the masses or even for another person may not be true for us. So it is very important not to go along with everybody because it is the popular thing to do. We need to experience the stillness within ourselves during meditation and hear God speaking to us alone. In this silence, we will always find the answer that is right for us and the peace that we are seeking.

On the other hand, we need to understand that others may not necessarily agree with our truths, but that is okay. We must allow others to be who they are and accept them, as long as they are not hurting anyone. If we accept them for who they are, they will be free to accomplish what they came here to do and then, they too will be at peace.

Creating Peace in Our Lives

We need to go beyond using our five senses in determining what we should do in so called "negative" situations, and allow ourselves to use our intuition to guide us through these experiences. Instead of going "out there" to determine what is needed, we need to go within ourselves. If we start listening to our intuition, we will always receive a peaceful response because we will be more in touch with our higher purpose.

Also, if we are attentive to our inner guidance, when negativity is sent our way, we will instantly send love in response to any negative energy. This does not mean we need to stay in situations that are negative just to avoid conflict. This means that we can send God's love to another if he or she is affecting us in a negative way, and then move on from that relationship.

After we have moved on from a relationship, we need to continue to send loving energy, release all resentment, and allow our inner selves to guide us through any further seemingly difficult situations with that person. If we hold onto anger or resentment, we are not only hurting the other person, but we are hurting ourselves as well.

Creating Peace Outside of Ourselves

As stated before, creating a peaceful world begins with creating peace within ourselves first. When we are at peace, we can then extend that peace so that it reaches out all over the world. The following are examples of what we can do to create peace *outside* of ourselves:

- Experiment for a few hours each day by not allowing anyone to disrupt the peace within yourself, no matter what another does. This may seem very difficult to accomplish at first. When you have mastered this for a few hours, you can try it for a full day, and then another. By refusing to allow anyone to disrupt your life, you will finally understand that you have total control of the peace you have within yourself. You will understand that it does not matter what happens on the outside that creates peace in your life, but rather, it's how you *react* to what goes on around you. And if you still find it difficult to maintain peace within yourself, all you need to do is to say a little prayer asking God and the angels to help you.
- Take three one-minute breaks every day. In the morning, before getting up, spend a minute "feeling" peace on earth. Imagine that *all* world leaders are cooperating to ensure global peace and harmony. Experience the new tranquility. If there is war, see all soldiers coming back home and being reunited with their families. Repeat this same visualization at lunchtime, and then right before bedtime. The important thing is to *feel* the peace as if it's happening right now.
- Also in the morning upon awakening and right before going to sleep, spend another minute visualizing hundreds of thousands of God's angels protecting the whole world. See their light and love. Feel their protection. Know they are always there working to insure peace on earth.
- Practice peace by being peaceful. Do not fight against war, but instead take a stand *for* peace. Fighting against *anything* or *anyone* is not peaceful at all. Remember that no problem is solved with the same type of energy that started it. Let us therefore extend only positive, peaceful energy out into this beautiful world.

- Create group meditations for world peace. Many studies have proven that when a group of individuals are brought together to pray for peace, there is a significant decrease in the number of violent crimes afterwards. For example, on February 2, 2003, hundreds of thousands of people joined together around the world to "bend" the world towards peace. This powerful event was called the "Great Experiment" and was organized by peace troubadour and author, James Twyman. The day after the vigil, there was a dramatic drop from 50%–100% in violent incidents throughout Israel and Palestine. Also, shots fired at military installations dropped by at least 50%.
- Avoid watching or reading negative news. The media tends to focus on the "bad stuff" so that it will sell newspapers and television space. Rely on your own inner guidance as to what you need to watch or read.
- To create peace in the world, you need to be at peace. Remember that what you focus on expands. You need to redirect your thoughts of fear and hate to thoughts of peace and compassion.

The Most Powerful Weapon Is Love

The most powerful weapon we have is our love, and with that weapon, we can wipe out any energy that is of a lower vibration, including hate, violence, greed, jealousy, or any other negative energy. Using negativity to wipe out negativity only reproduces the same energy. The only way to dispel the darkness is to shine light upon it. This goes for situations within ourselves, towards others, and even in far larger situations, such as in worldly conflicts.

Let each of us make a conscious choice to make the world a better place in which to live. As the song says, "Let there be peace on earth, and let it begin with me." Let us all throw down our weapons and offer the olive branch to our fellow man from this point on.

May peace prevail on earth!

Conclusion

Thank you so much for accompanying me on my spiritual journey. Even after I had finished this book, I was still receiving wonderful messages from the angels and deceased loved ones. Although I wanted to include them all, I had to end somewhere.

I hope you now understand that there really is much more to life than just what is on the surface. Go within yourself and you will find all you need to know there. Meditate regularly, create peace in the world around you, and remember who you are. God and His angels are there for you and always have been. Your loved ones who have crossed over are okay and will go to any length to let you know that. They want you to laugh and not grieve for them. The rainbow follows the storm and all is well.

And so it is. I love you and may peace be with you now and always!

Peace Meditation

Love is a fruit, in season at all times and within the reach of every hand. Anyone may gather it and no limit is set. Everyone can reach this love through meditation.

—Mother Theresa

The following is a guided meditation for peace. This meditation can be used either in a group or individual setting. You may wish to record this meditation using your own voice with soothing music in the background for maximum effectiveness.

Go into a room where you will not be disturbed for about twenty minutes. Turn off the phone or whatever else that would distract you from completely relaxing. This is going to be your time to relax and feel the peace within you. Okay, good.

Sit down in a comfortable position. Allow your feet to be flat on the floor and make sure your spine is straight. Begin by doing the Edgar Cayce head and neck exercises. Slowly drop your chin to your chest and the raise it back up to normal position. Do this three times. (pause) Now drop your head all the way back and raise it up to normal position. Do this three times. (pause) Drop your right ear to your right shoulder and then bring your head back up to normal position three times. (pause) Now do the same thing on the other side. Drop your left ear to your left shoulder and then bring it back up three times. (pause) Now drop your chin to your chest and now slowly circle your head all the way around towards the right three times. (pause) Now this time, drop your head to your chest and circle your head three times going towards the left. (pause)

155

Let us now do our deep breathing exercises. Use your left index finger to close your left nostril and inhale deeply through your right nostril. Exhale fully and completely through your mouth. Do this three times. (pause) Now using your right index finger, close your right nostril and inhale through your left nostril. Now use your left index finger and close your left nostril and exhale through your right nostril. Do this three times. (pause) Good!

Now you may close your eyes and imagine you are going inside the center of your feet. Feel yourself in your feet and then tense them as hard as you can for a count of three. Now relax them. Good! Now move up to the inside of your ankles and the lower part of your legs. Tense and relax them. Move up to your knees and tense them as hard as you can and then let it go. Move up a little further to your upper legs and thighs and tense them hard for a count of three and then relax them. Now move up a little further and tense your buttocks for a count of three and then relax these muscles. Keep moving up and tense and relax your lower back and stomach. Good! Now move up to your upper back and chest area. Tense them as hard as you can, and then relax them. Great! Now go into your hands and fingers, and tense them hard. Now release these muscles. Move up to your lower arms and tense and then relax them. Now go up to your upper arms, and tense and relax them. Next, raise your shoulders as high as you can and tense them. Now lower them to normal position and relax these muscles. Move up into your facial area and tighten the muscles on your face. Hold these muscles tight for three seconds and then relax them. Very good!

Now just feel your body relaxing even further. Notice if there are any knots or glitches, and go inside each one, dissolving any tension or negative energy. Take your time. I will wait. (pause)

Now I want you to drift away, float away, higher and higher, up, up, into the heavens, to another place far, far away. You feel yourself drifting slowly at first. (pause) Wonderful! Now you're picking up the pace and moving faster and faster. You now are becoming aware of *just how vast the universe really is as you fly past the stars, planets, and multiple galaxies. You are in awe at the beauty of it all.*

Okay, you are now being guided to slow down. You are moving slower and slower and feel yourself being drawn to a particular planet. You land on this planet, and in an instant you feel total peace and tranquility. This is a place where there is nothing to worry about. A place where love is all there is. You are in paradise. You love everyone and everyone loves you too. This is a place where there is complete and total harmony. There are no struggles, only peace and love. Here you are able to feel the oneness of all of life and you no longer feel separate from anyone else. You are able to see how everything and everyone is connected.

You realize that the peace that you yearn for on earth begins with the peace you are feeling inside yourself right now. You desire to always feel this wonderful peace and want to bring it back and share it with those on earth. With that thought, a beautiful light appears before you. Although you didn't think it was possible, you now experience an even deeper knowing, a deeper peace than you have ever experienced before. The light turns into the form of a beautiful angel and she tells you that she is giving you a gift. Your wish has been granted and you will be able to take this peace and knowingness back to your beautiful planet earth when you return there. You are so thankful for this miracle, and then the angel tells you she will never leave you. With this knowingness, you embrace the angel, and then together you begin to move again.

You start moving slowly, and then gradually you pick up your pace. Faster and faster, you rush past millions of stars and galaxies as you head back towards your home, planet earth. As you finally approach the planet earth again, you begin to slow down. You are moving slower and slower, and you finally come to a halt right outside the earth's atmosphere. From where you are, you see a beautiful spark of light emanating from the center of the earth. You watch this light expanding more and more, until it covers the whole world, and you feel the light cleansing it, creating the same total peace that you have found across the universe on the planet that you have just visited. Now you see the light expanding even further—out, out into the universe. Now the whole universe feels this total peace. What a blessing from the heavens!

You now begin to circle the entire planet and you have a wonderful vision of all the world leaders standing peacefully together in one place. From the heavens, they are each being given the understanding of the urgency of peace on earth now. You see all world leaders in agreement in admitting that war is a mistake and will never happen again. See all sides meeting and agreeing to do whatever is necessary to allow peace to prevail. Everyone is sorry that they did not understand how their negative actions had affected the earth before. They each forgive one another, and then they also forgive themselves. See this happening for each leader, one by one. (pause) Everyone wonders why this couldn't have been done before. Everyone is relieved; now they know peace. They now know without a doubt that this is the way the world is supposed to be. There are no more egos saying, "I am better than you" or "I know what's best for the world." Now there is cooperation, not competition. The world is at peace! (pause)

See now how positive thought forms all over the world are joining together and expanding, and all negative thought forms are being dissolved. These positive thought forms are creating peace within each person and are expanding out to family, friends, neighbors, coworkers, and throughout each city, state, country, continent, the world, and the entire universe as well.

Archangel Michael now appears before you as God's messenger and informs you that this is really happening now. He's now asking you to begin a new way of thinking. From now on, he's asking you to send love in response to every situation. He's asking you not to let anyone offend you, no matter what they do. He's now showing you the ripple effect of the love you will be sending out ... how you will be affecting the whole world just by changing your thoughts.

He's telling you to continue to pray for peace and to know that your prayers will be answered.

Now he's giving you the knowledge that, although we are all one, you are unique in your oneness. Listen to the truth within yourself. Remember who you are and remember what you came on earth to do. In your stillness, now feel what you need to do to allow this peace to remain within you each and every day. (pause)

Archangel Michael is now asking you to take three one-minute breaks each day: one in the morning when you wake up, one at lunchtime, and one before you go to sleep. During these breaks, he wants you to experience this same wonderful peace that you are feeling right now.

Now see hundreds of thousands of angels protecting the earth, sending it light, love, and peace. Feel it and know this is happening now. You thank the angels for their never-ending protection. (pause)

You suddenly remember to also thank the magnificent angel who allowed you to bring this beautiful gift of peace to earth. (pause) You now thank Archangel Michael for delivering God's messages on how to maintain this peace. (pause) And now, at this time, you say good-bye to the angels, knowing if you ever need them, they will immediately be there for you again. (pause)

Okay, good! Now take a nice deep breath and become aware again of the room in which you are sitting. (pause) Gradually feel yourself reanimate your body. (pause) Slowly move your fingers and your toes. Stretch out your arms and your legs as far as they will go. Excellent!

And when you are ready, you may open your eyes, and become wide awake, knowing that there is nothing BUT peace, both within yourself and in the world as well!

Peace Prayers and Organizations

The fruit of silence is prayer;
the fruit of prayer is faith;
the fruit of faith is love;
the fruit of love is service;
the fruit of service is peace.

—Mother Teresa

The following are prayers dedicated to maintaining peace on earth. When you say these prayers, feel and know that they are being answered now. Do not beg God for peace, for that would mean that you do not believe He will answer your prayers. Remember, it's the energy from true faith that allows your prayers to be answered.

Prayer for Raising the Consciousness of the Planet

Dearest God, please allow all of us on earth to rise to a higher level of consciousness where only peace prevails on earth. Help us release all negative and fearful energy now. Allow us to see Your love within each person. Take away all negativity that blinds us from experiencing this total love.

Please release negativity from all world leaders. Help them to release the energy that makes them want to conquer another country. Clear away their desire to attack and go to war. Please allow world leaders to see that love and forgiveness are the most powerful weap-

ons, and from this point on, allow only leaders who will maintain peace to remain in a position of power.

Allow your love to dispel all negativity from everyone involved in terrorist activities. Let this love permeate them now so that they will never want to hurt anyone ever again.

Grant peace to all earthbound spirits who died in acts of terrorism. Please extend this peace to their families and friends as well. Release any cords that are binding them to the pain they or their loved ones have experienced from these terrorist acts. Please set them free and take away all their suffering right now. Thank you.

Let your love shine through in the media, so that love and peace are the main focus, not war and violence. Allow those in the media to understand that they bring more energy to what they cover, so allow them to deliberately cover peaceful, positive events that make people feel good.

God, please surround the earth with thousands of your angels to help protect our beautiful planet. Thank you for these wonderful helpers and messengers of light who are always there for us, sending us so much love and light.

We now call upon the archangels. We first ask Archangel Michael to help remove all negative energy from our planet. Michael, please help us to remove the negativity within ourselves first, enabling us to feel only peace within ourselves. We now ask you to remove all negativity from the leaders of the world and the entire mass consciousness.

We now call upon Archangel Gabriel. Gabriel, please help us to peacefully and effectively communicate our needs to others, allowing only positive words to be spoken by all of us, especially our world's leaders. We also ask you to allow us all to see that effective communication is the first step in creating peace both within ourselves and the world as well.

We now call upon Archangel Uriel and ask him to please help us to maintain this peace. Uriel, we also ask you to allow only those who are peacemakers to remain in a position of power from this point on. We ask you also to help, protect, and motivate all lightworkers to spread this message of love and peace, thereby causing a new ripple effect of positive energy across the world.

We finally call upon Archangel Raphael and ask him to heal our planet from all past actions that have affected the world in a negative way. Raphael, we also ask you to replace all negative thoughtforms with positive ones and surround our planet with the healing, white light of God.

We thank you God and all your wonderful angels for allowing us to experience only peace from this point on. We are sorry for the error of our ways in the past, but that is all behind us now. For at this time and forevermore, peace prevails on earth.

And so it is!

Prayer to Create Peace Within

Dear God, help me to release anything that I am holding onto that is preventing me from experiencing your total peace. At this moment, help me to forgive everyone who has hurt me in any way. Also help me to forgive myself for those times when I have been less than perfect. Assist me in understanding the concept that anything besides love is just an illusion. With this new-found understanding, allow me to see that I can release everything within myself that is blocking this love right now. As I find peace within myself, help me extend it and become an instrument of this peace to the world. I adore you and thank you so much. Amen.

Prayer to Become an Instrument of Peace

God, please show me what I can do to become an instrument of your peace. Guide me to perfect situations each and every day where I may be of service to my fellow man. Assist me in putting my ego aside so I may fully be able to see the needs of others. In coming to the aid of my fellow man, I am helping you, God, and I'm helping myself as well. Allow me to give as freely to others as you have given freely to me. Help me to respond to every situation with your Divine love.

*Thank you so much, God, for granting me your perfect knowledge
and strength so that I may always know what I need to do to maintain
peace on earth. Amen.*

Peace Prayers of Major Religions

Whenever I hold peace meditations, I love to incorporate
the following peace prayers from various religions. During these
meditations, I place eleven candles around the room (one for
each major religion). I then ask each person who is there to read
one prayer and light a corresponding candle for it. These prayers
show that we are all in agreement in desiring peace on our
magnificent planet!

The Baha'i for Peace

Be generous in prosperity and thankful in adversity.
Be fair in thy judgment, and guarded in thy speech.
Be a lamp unto those who walk in darkness, and a home to the
*   stranger.*
Be eyes to the blind, and a guiding light unto the feet of the erring.
Be a breath of life to the body of humankind, a dew upon the soil
*   of the human heart,*
and a fruit upon the tree of humility.

Buddhist Prayer for Peace

May all beings everywhere plagued with sufferings of body and
mind quickly be freed from their illnesses.
May those frightened cease to be afraid
and may those bound be free.
May the powerless find power,
and may people think of befriending one another.
May those who find themselves in trackless,
fearful wildernesses—the children, the aged, the unprotected—

be guarded by beneficent celestials,
and may they quickly attain Buddhahood.

Christian Prayer for Peace

Blessed are the Peacemakers
for they shall be known as the Children of God.
But I say to you that hear, love your enemies, do good to those
who hate you, bless those who curse you, pray for those who
abuse you.
To those who strike you on the cheek, offer the other also, and
from those who take away your cloak, do not withhold your coat
as well.
Give to everyone who begs from you, and of those who take
away your goods, do not ask for them again.
And as you wish that others would to do you,
do so to them.

Hindu Prayer for Peace

Oh God, lead us from the unreal to the real.
Oh God, lead us from darkness to light.
Oh God, lead us from death to immortality.
Shanti, Shanti, Shanti unto all.

Oh Lord God Almighty, may there be peace in celestial regions.
May there be peace on earth.
May the waters be appeasing.
May herbs be wholesome, and may trees and plants bring peace
    to all.
May all beneficent beings bring peace to us.
May thy Vedic Law propagate peace all through the world.
May all things be a source of peace to us.

And may thy peace itself bestow peace on all.
And may that peace come to me also.

Jainist Prayer for Peace

Peace and Universal Love is the essence of the Gospel preached
by all the Enlightened Ones.
The Lord has preached that equanimity is the Dharma.
Forgive do I, creatures all,
and let all creatures forgive me.
Unto all have I amity, and unto none enmity.
Know that violence is the root cause of all miseries in the world.
Violence in fact, is the knot of bondage.

"Do not injure any living being."
This is the eternal, perennial, and unalterable
way of spiritual life.

A weapon, howsoever powerful it may be,
can always be superseded by a superior one;
but no weapon can, however,
be superior to non-violence and love.

Jewish Prayer for Peace

Come let us go up to the mountain of the Lord, that we may walk
the paths of the most high.
And we shall beat our swords into ploughshares, and our spears
into pruning hooks.
Nations shall not lift up sword against nation—neither shall they
learn war any more.
And none shall be afraid, for the mouth of the Lord of Hosts has
spoken.

Muslim Prayer for Peace

In the name of Allah the beneficent, the merciful, praise be to
the Lord of the Universe, who has created us and made us into
tribes and nations that we may know each other, not that we
may despise each other.
If the enemy incline towards peace, do thou also incline towards
peace, and trust God, for the Lord is the one that heareth and
knoweth all things.
And the servants of God, most Gracious, are those who walk on
the earth in humility, and when we address them, we say
"Peace."

Native African Prayer for Peace

Almighty God, the Great Thumb
we cannot evade to tie any knot.
The Roaring Thunder that splits mighty trees;
the all-seeing Lord up on high who sees
even the footprints of an antelope on a rock mass here on earth.
You are the one who does not hesitate to respond to our call.
You are the cornerstone of peace.

Native American Prayer for Peace

Oh Great Spirit of our ancestors, I raise my pipe to you;
To your messengers in the four winds, and
to Mother Earth who provides for your children.
Give us the wisdom to teach our children to love, to respect, and
to be kind to each other, so that they may grow with peace in
    mind.
Let us learn to share all good things that you provide for us on this
    earth.

Shinto Prayer for Peace

Although the people living across the ocean surrounding us
I believe are all our brothers and sisters, why are there
constant troubles in the world?
Why do winds and waves rise in the ocean surrounding us?
I only earnestly wish that the wind will soon puff away all the
clouds which are hanging over the tops of the mountains.

Zoroastrian Prayer for Peace

We pray to God to eradicate all the misery in the world.
that understanding triumph over ignorance,
that generosity triumph over indifference,
that trust triumph over contempt, and
that truth triumph over falsehood.

Peace Organizations

Below are some links to peace organizations. I encourage you to check out these wonderful sites:

The World Peace Prayer Society *has several ongoing peace projects, among them*
peace pole planting (over 100,000 world wide).
Telephone: 212-755-4755
www.worldpeace.org

Pathways to Peace *ignites the collective will of humanity to make peace a practical reality and to build cooperation among existing organizations and programs which demonstrate peace in its multifold expressions.*
Telephone: 415-461-0500
http://pathwaystopeace.org

Center for the Advancement of Nonviolence *is sponsor of the Season for Nonviolence in L.A., an international commemoration of Mahatma Gandhi and Martin Luther King that demonstrates how nonviolence can heal, transform, and empower our lives and communities.*
1223 Wilshire Blvd. #472, Santa Monica, CA 90403
www.nonviolenceworks.com

The Fellowship of Reconciliation, *the largest and oldest interfaith peace organization in the U.S., holds a vision of a beloved community in which differences are respected, conflicts are addressed nonviolently, oppressive structures are dismantled, and people live in harmony with the earth. FOR offers a resource packet for responding to 9/11, hate crimes, and the US military campaign. Ongoing projects include a campaign against the Iraqi sanctions and for the abolition of nuclear weapons. FOR also sends delegations to Israel/Palestine,* *works for economic justice, and honors those working for social change through nonviolent means with the Pfeffer Peace Prize and the MLK Award.*

    P.O. Box 271, Nyack, NY 10960

    Telephone: 845-358-4601

    www.forusa.org

Season for Non Violence

A season for nonviolence, January 30–April 4, is a national 64-day educational, media, and grass-roots campaign dedicated to demonstrating that nonviolence is a powerful way to heal, transform, and empower our lives and our communities. Inspired by the 50th and 30th memorial anniversaries of Mahatma Gandhi and Martin Luther King, this international event honors their vision for an empowered, nonviolent world. The Association for Global New Thought is the convening organization.

    1514 Main St. #2, Evanston, IL 06202

    Telephone: 847-866-9525

    www.agnt.org/snv02.htm

Photo by Steve Belner

About
the Author

Karen was sitting on the edge of her bed, suffering from a high fever and bronchitis, when a beautiful white light appeared in the room and slowly floated towards her. She knew she could speak to it and silently demanded, "If you are not of God, you must leave." In spite of her request, the light continued to move closer, and it finally enveloped her, bestowing upon her a feeling of total peace, a tranquility she never felt before. The light spoke directly to her in Italian, whispering, "*Luce lucina, bella luce lucina.*" Since her grandparents were Italian, she knew what the words meant—"Light, little light, beautiful little light." She was speechless, and tears of joy rolled down her face. From that moment on, her life was never the same, and she now receives very specific messages from angels and deceased loved ones on a regular basis.

Karen is a Certified Spiritual Counselor (certified by author Doreen Virtue), a Usui and Lightarian Reiki Master and Energy Healer, a Certified Hypnotherapist, and a Past Life Regressionist. She has earned her Bachelor of Arts Degree from Boston University and her Masters Degree in Business from Fordham University.

Her stories can be found in the A.R.E.'s *Venture Inward Magazine,* and also in Dr. Doreen Virtue's angel books, *Healing with the Angels, Angel Visions,* and *Earth Angels.*

For more information on Karen or her workshops, you can visit her at www.lucelucina.com.